What I
Have
Seen

What I Have Seen

Darrell "Buzz" Malcolm

To order additional copies of this book, contact:
Xlibris
1-888-795-4274
www.Xlibris.com
Orders@Xlibris.com
793836

CONTENTS

Branches

Outside the window I did see
A branch on an oak tree
Twisting and turning it reached out you see
Shades of brown and woody the branch it be

Upon the sturdy branch others stretched forth
Smaller in size they stretch to the sky
Some branching out again stretching from where they came
With others they define the tree as a beautiful bouquet

A symbol of strength is the mighty tree
With many branches spreading far and wide
Providing homes for those that reside inside
And food for those that need, it provides

Leaves of green attached to the branches
Providing shade and shelter which others match
Reaching out to the sky above
A gesture of God's Everlasting Love

But we are the branches and leaves of God's tree
Nourished from the Son you see
To stretch forth into the world everyday
To be disciples of the Almighty God, and to follow His Way

Thank You God for being our tree of life

Buzz

There are several meanings to this verse, if you desire to take it apart.

One is the church, from it early beginnings, how it grows and spreads it message to the world.

A second the Bible as it spreads through out the land.

Third are the followers of the Way and how he or she spreads the Word or actions in his or her daily life.

Some of us are branches small and short that try our best to follow the Way.

Others are much larger branches that bare much fruit with many branches that come from one sturdy branch.

Art was the later.

A Christian that was concerned about others and cared for others in his own special way.

A strong branch that grew many branches:

branches of caring, hope, comfort, compassion, service and many more.
A strong branch that bore much fruit and fruit to come.

I had this idea before Art memorial service and while at the service waiting for it to being I put a lot of my ideas down on paper. Went home with more of the memorial service in mind and composed the verse "Branches" with Art in mind.

A Bridge

A unique structure that expands the way
We may pass over or under most everyday
Over a deep craves or a shallow stream
Maybe an engineer's lofty dream

They extend over water wide and deep
Provide passage over a creek for the sheep
Over the highway to help the wildlife survive
Providing a life line to the other side

Some bridges link town to town
Unfortunately some old bridges have fallen down
Civil Rights have made a bridge a part of history
Other new shiny and bright; serve us all, others a unique mystery

We play a game that goes on and on
Some play weekly with friends, some very long
There is a children's game of a bridge long gone
That stands today in Lake Havasu, proud and strong

Yet there is a bridge we tend to forget
Some say the bridge was definitely a misfit
It has existed for many a year
Transporting people to a life of little fear

For this bridge is God's only Son
With our passage, are sins are done
Bridging the gap; from death to life
Leading us over to a new life, clear and bright

Thank You God for Your Son, the bridge to new life

Buzz

A Butterfly

Working outside the other day
Cleaning up old and dead branches and leaves
Things that could get in the plants growing way
Giving them some water and food on this Spring day

A time to rest, I sat by a lilac bush
Its flowers in bunches of purple and white
Swaying gently in the Spring breeze
As their sweet aroma filled the air

The aroma was calming and pleasant to me
Filling my mind with a relaxing peace
For at the present my mind was on that lilac bush
With blossoms reaching to the Heaven above

A visitor approached this lilac bush
I know not from where it came
But this black and orange butterfly did appear
Flitting from blossoms to blossoms so near

I believe he, maybe she, was searching for food
Drawing nectar a little at a time
Sampling one blossom then the next
The butterfly would land then fold its wings

Pause for a moment to feed and unfold its wings
Then on to the next blossom it went
Repeating the process again and again
Then flitting to the other side of the bush it went

God created that butterfly I did see
And the lilac bush of purple and white
To bring sweet aroma through the Spring breeze
And nectar to a hungry butterfly you see

We are all part of God's Creation
Be it lilac bush or butterfly or me
All with a purpose and that would be
To praise God a beautiful relationship you see

Thank you God for that little bit of nature I did see

Buzz

A Card

Received a card the other day
Nothing really special as it came its' way
Paper and ink of colors it did display
Bearing a greeting the words it did say

Cards come in many sizes and shapes
Filling with pictures and words that are all related
In many a color and design
All from a person that has you in mind

Birthday cards come and go
Telling us that we may be getting old
Saying another year has passed
Some giving us a time to laugh

The cards I enjoy the most come late in the year
For they tell us Christmas is near
A time to celebrate the birth of Immanuel
An event that should not be annual

They come with many designs you see
Mangers, Wisemen, birds, even a Christmas tree
Telling a story that happened long ago
In a land far away that I do not know

Telling us the message of the event
Of a babe that God sent
To bring light to all the nations
Showing us a new life with great elation

For the cards come from those who care
Sharing love and experience they would share
Of a common bond they all enjoy
Of love and the birth of God's baby boy

**Thank You God for Christmas Cards and
their true Christmas message**

Buzz

A Curious Sight

What a curious sight out my window I did see
High in the branches of an oak tree
For winter was here and most of the leaves had fallen away
Those that were left were crinkled and brown

There was not a breeze that I could see
For the leaves on the tree were as still as could be
Yet one leaf was different from the rest
It captured my eyes as I sat at my desk

This leaf on that tree would swing and sway
Back and forth on that branch it did move this day
Back and forth like a pendulum swinging
Then slowly, it would slow down to be as still as the rest

I though it was done with its moving about
Then it began to swing and sway again all around
Back and forth as if to say
What joy I am having as I swing this way

I watched the leaf for a very long time
Swing on that branch so high in that tree
With the other leaves as still as could be
It looked as if it were singing a song

God's world of Nature is a wondrous thing
Beauty and wonder in a single leaf's swing
Swinging and swaying with no breeze to be seen
Was it glorifying God with its rhythmic swing?

Thank you God for so simple a thing as a single leaf swinging

Buzz

A Day outside in Spring time

A Spring day is a day to behold
The ever changing scene never gets old
Under sky of blue Spring is here to stay
As clouds pass lazily on their way

The gentle breeze moves the new leaves around
As the breeze makes a frequent rushing sound
Gently moving the trees and bushes to and fro
And carrying new pollen to the plants and the ground below

Sounds are different in the Spring
As we hear birds chatter on the wing
Telling of the places they have been
And the new lives they are about to begin

A new aroma has begun to fill the air
For the purple lilacs are blooming there
Clusters upon clusters fill the branches high
Enticing us to enjoy their delicate flowers as we pass by

For outside in Spring many things can be seem
A much different scene than the Winter scene
For green in many shades we do see
Covering the once brown land from branch to grass to trees

We enjoy the sight of Spring
The warmth of the sun to everything
Filling the days with the promises of more to come
For now we know that Winter is done

For out of the dominate time of Winter has come
New life as Spring has begun
Spring is resurrection time
Out of death comes life and Love Divine

Our Savior, years ago left death behind
Planting a new message in our mind
To be kind and compassionate to all mankind
By following the example of Love Devine

**Thank You God for the time outside we
have to see Your Spring time**

Buzz

The Dogwood Tree

We planted a dogwood a few years ago
To celebrate a couple of lives we all knew
To grow in memory of those two
Who raised a family so true

We scatted their ashes at the base of the tree
To nourish the new sapling to help it be
A strong and beautiful dogwood tree
And remind us of the lives they had with you and me

We put a fence around that tree
To protect it from the animals that feed
Of the nourishing leaves of that dogwood tree
Nourished from the love they gave to you and me

God took them away several years ago
Part of them live in that tree we love so
Through winter storms and baking sun
With blooming white flowers so much fun

Although in Heaven they do reside
With loved ones they know side by side
For their memories are there in that tree so glad
Gracing the land with memories so grand

Thank You God for the memories from our dogwood tree

Buzz

A Door

Sitting in the living room I saw familiar things
Chairs, tables, books, papers and more
What caught my attention this day was the door
A device that lets us do many things

It lets us go out the world to see
Or in to the comfort and security be
Shapes and sizes they vary so much
Elegant and plain they are to the touch

But I remember a scene of a door I did see
A stained glass window of a door it be
A man in a long robe was standing there
Waiting next to a weathered wooden door

This door was unique, as I looked closer that day
There was no outside latch on that door I would say
How could He enter through a door so closed?
For that door must be opened from the other side you know

For I am on the other side of that door
Do I open that door and let Him in
Or ignore that knocking and not let Him enter within
For it may be a stranger that I do not want here

Reluctantly I answered the door and let Him in
We exchanged pleasantries and sat down for tea
He was pleasant and serene and His voice calmed me down
For His voice and manners lit up the room
with warmth before unknown

In an hour or two the conversation was eventually about me
For He saw within me sins on that day
He told me if I believed in Him and followed His Way
He would forgive me my sins today and always

We finished that day with a small meal of fish, bread and wine
That He did bless as we sat down to dine and pray
An inner peace I did have that special day
I asked Him to stay but He had to be on His Way

I was glad that I opened the door that day
For now I do follow Him and follow His Way
Filled with peace for my sins are gone
Forever I am with The Holy Father's Son and to Him I belong

We all need to answer that knock on the door
To let Him come in and learn of His Way
For with Him will come peace on that day
The door with no outside latch can be the Way

Thank You God for the opening of that door.

Buzz

A Fall Carpet (A Coat of Many Colors)

The world outside changes every day
For a new day is now on display
A new carpet covered the ground
Fall leaves carpet the ground all around

For now I see a yellow-green carpet
The color so bright and so profound
Above the carpet a tree; as bare as bare can be
For the Fall has given this scene to me

Looking around other carpets I do see
Covering the ground in glorious splendor be
Carpets of red from the Liquid Amber tree
A bright yellow carpet from the Quaking Aspin I see

Created by the Fall as temperatures go down
Breezes that shuffle the leaves around
The sun as it glides lower in the sky
Lengthening the night as it is shortening the day's light

The many colored carpets are a wonderful thing
Protecting the ground until spring
Providing shelter from coolness of the night
Coloring the world to make it beautiful and bright

We enjoy this Fall season Whom God has brought
For colors that brighten the day
Tell us change is on its' way
Giving thanks for the world on display

God gave us the carpet I see
Protecting the ground when winter be
Planting the seeds that grow in the spring
Protecting the seeds from Winter's sting

For the Fall and Winter are times to reflect
On the bounty Whom God has provided, His best
For our faith is what pulls us through
The darkness of times when we are blue

Like the leafy carpet of Fall that covers the ground
God's Grace and assistance is like a coat that is all around
Providing us with warmth and protection day after day
As we follow the teaching of His Son and His Way

**Thank You God for the beauty and
significance of the season of Fall**

Buzz

A Frame

A frame is a unique device
Surrounding a picture very nice
Some as plain as can be
Others very ornate and fancy you see

Size can vary from very small to very large they be
Windows in a house large to small through which we see
On the walls around our rooms
Pictures of many sizes in glory they loom

They usually come with sides of four
Like the frame of a door
Most any shape can be a frame
Showing it subject in glorious fame

We see frames most everywhere
Around a clock or on a building over there
Just look around and you will see
Frames where ever you may be

There is a special frame I have in mind
Four sides and really quit divine
God, Jesus, the Bible and Holy Spirit they be
A holy frame that surrounds you and me

Within that frame are words of love
Delivered to you and me by a dove
"Eternal, everlasting Love from Me to you"
Its frame stretching beyond the never-ending blue.

Thank You God for Your holy frame that surrounds us

Buzz

A Garden

A garden is a special place
For there are many kinds they say
Some larger than you can walk in a day
Others a box on a widow sill where they stay

They come in many a varieties
Vegetables, flowers, ornamental or plain
Some with fountains, tables and benches
Others with paths that wind, and others paths straight

Most of them a place to enjoy
The nature around in slow-mo
Serene and quiet and a comfort they be
Slowing down the world inside you and me

There are famous gardens far and wide
The Garden of Eden is one I recall
The Garden of the gods a rocky place it be
Or the aroma of a rose garden close to me

Special places set aside
Carved out of places busy and wide
Filling a void they comfort and provide
A place to commune with nature and me inside

But there is one garden I would like to see
A garden of long ago yet I can still foresee
It had a special guest many years ago
He came alone yet followed by His friends and a foe

They came after the evening sun had set
Full from a Passover meal they had earlier partaken
To that garden with shadows so dark and gray
For He came from the meal to pray

He prayed to His Father above that night
For strength to endure the trial quickly in sight
Three times He did ask them to stay with Him there
For the day had been long and a night they could not bare

Then out of the darkness lights did appear
Bringing with it guards that drew ever so near
To take Him away in the gloom of the night
His followers all fled in fear of that sight

The garden is now a peaceful place
Yet filled with the memories of that dreadful act that day
That took away an innocent man
He died for you and me as no other man can

He was laid in a garden tomb a short distance away
Only to leave in His own triumphant way
To join His Father in Heaven above
For He died for our sins, for us He did love

For a garden is a special place you know
A place of peaceful tranquility and so
Where nature slows the world around
And where God reveals His everlasting presence

Thank You God for the peace of a garden serene

Buzz

A Gate

A gate is an interesting thing
Hanging on a fence it is free to swing
Letting things venture in and out
An opening in a fence is what a gate is all about

A gate has many sizes and shapes you see
Some tall, some wide, or narrow and some need a key
Other ornate with iron works fancy as can be
Still others but wires attached to a tree

They provide a job to keep us safe
Away from a dangerous place
Or letting us in, to enjoy some fun
Where we can relax or run

For the fence is like a wall
And the wall is your sin; it may be short or quite tall
To put the wall behind us and remove your sin
Through the gatekeeper you must pass to win

We must ask the gatekeeper to let us pass through
And have the sin some old and some new
Behind us to start a new day
For only the gatekeeper has a new Way

He asked but one question before you may pass
'Do you believe in Me' to leave the past
For the gatekeeper knows all you have done
Be it good or bad and what you thought was fun

Through the gate life may not be easier
But by our side the gatekeeper is always near
Helping us along the way
To a bright and joyful day

Thank You God for gates and Your Son the Gatekeeper

Buzz

A Hammer

I am a humble tool
Made of forged steel with a fiberglass handle
With cousins that come in many sizes
Shapes and purposes to be used

My particular head design has a blunt end
With a curved forged claw on the other
My handle being fiberglass is about a foot long
Wrapped in rubber for a better grip

Working hard most of the day
Pounding nails to make the project sturdy
I have pounded many a nail hard and fast
Hopefully making the project last

My family used to be king
Fastening many a thing
Until they came along
Phillips and slot head the screw brothers

There was a cousin long, long ago
He was a Roman hammer they say
That worked in a land far, far away
In a time I do not know

As the story goes; passed down to me
He had an important job that day
Three prisoners were to be nailed to a cross
On a hill not that far away

He said he saw them slowly walking
Dragging their wooden crosses up the hill
At the top of the hill the soldiers removed their garments
Laid them down on the crosses on the ground

He said his job was simple that day
To hit a long nail into the wrist and feet of the man
He said he struck the nail as true as can be
Three or four hits all that it took

Two of the prisoners did struggle a bit
But true to his form he hit the nails true
Knowing the day was almost done
Only one prisoner was left to do

This man was different than the other two
He did not struggle as the others did
He saw agony in His face as he struck the nails true
Wanting to say he did not want this for You

He finished the job with blood on his face
Knowing his job was done that day
Hitting the ground he wondered what he had done
For this man he heard had done nothing wrong

He said he was used many times more
But could not forget that man that day
He knew He was innocent
For a strange feeling came over him and stayed

He said he heard later that the man who died that day
Rose from the dead, a miracle they say
That He died for the sins of the world
And saved mankind to follow His way

The Roman hammer has long passed away
For he left us a story we pass on today
Of a man who died that faithful day
Who took all of mankind's sin away

No matter how small or large we be
God has a time and place for thee
A part of a plan He's had all along
To guide and protect thee all the day long

**God Thank You for those little things in life
that become significant with You**

Buzz

A House or Home

They define a house as a structure where people live
A home is define the same way they say
Yet to me a house is a structure you can live within
Home, a warm sanctuary where family and I can lay our heads

A house is a structure where people or animals can reside
They come in many shapes and sizes: tall, short, narrow or wide
Some with many rooms and some with one or two
Designs are varied from place to place all unique in many ways

A home on the other hand is all the above
But has a special sense to it's being
They are warm inside from wall to wall
Loaded with knickknacks and memories untold

The items are not special to you, only to me
Unique in their placement on a shelf or settee
A sanctuary from the outside world they be
Filled with comfort and a place I can be me

I have moved from place to place several times
Lived in houses for a while, sometimes on a dime
But then they became homes so dear
When familiar items appeared and family settled in here

Home is a place hard to describe
A full felling you get deep, deep inside
You carried it with you when venturing outside
Knowing it is still there when venture back to reside

We call the Church the House of the Lord
But it is more than a building to me
For within the walls are more than the eyes can see
Love, friends, compassion and Thee

Thank you God for family and homes.

Buzz

A January Day

A January day may be cold or bright
Bathed in the winter's light
Or cold from the winter's blustery wind
Chilling the body to the very skin

Some days are as bright as can be
As the sun reflects off the snowy sea
For high in the mountains the snow is deep
For skiing in the snow for some, so neat

January brings snow on the mountains high
As the snow capped peaks touch the sky
But down in the valley the rain does fall
As rain makes its frequent call

The rain makes the day a drizzly day
Some people like to go out and play
But most stay in and watch the rain go by
And wait for the rain to pass for the clear blue sky

God gave us the rain and snow
And the cold winter winds to blow
To give us time to think
How time passes in just a blink

That the only constant in life we enjoy
Is the love God does employ
For in January be the day cold, gloomy or bright
His Son is the warming light

Alight that takes the gloom away
For the Son is here every day
Filled with love, always on display
For with Him there is never a gloomy January day

**Thank You God for the January be it gloomy
or bright it's filled with Your Love**

Buzz

A Leaf

From my window I can see a spectular event
The changing of the seasons before my very eyes
One day as green as green as can be
The next day tints of yellow dot the trees

As days pass the green slowly fades away
Leaves of green replaced by leaves of yellow and brown
Other trees display other colors of red and gold
Then the leaves will slowly leave the tree

For gravity will taken its toll
Pulling the leaves to the ground below
Carpeting the ground with its coat of yellow, red and gold
Some will be scattered and move by the wind that does blow

Some leaves hang on a long as they can
Until a gust of autumn wind guides they slowly to the ground
More and more leaves cover and protect the ground below
For winter will approach with its cold and blanket of snow

Beneath the carpet of leaves life is there
Seeds from the oak tree are protected from the winter blast
Waiting for the winter to pass
Wondering when the spring sun will come to last

God gave us this season of fall
To put in our minds the glory of it all
That in the beauty of the falling leaves
We are protected and loved if we only believe

The leaves are a blanket that protects the ground
Like God's love that protects us so profound
Surrounding us with His love every day
And guiding us in a glorious Way

**Thank you God for the seasons it beauty
and protection You provide**

Buzz

A Liquid Amber Tree

I looked at a tree the other day
Standing tall stretching Heaven's way
Filling the sky with its leaves of green
Bending so slightly as a breeze made it lean

Covered with green leaves each in the shape of a star
A real middle green you can see from afar
The branches are like twisted ridges of rope
With small ridges like gray-brown walls above a castle mote

These ridges are scattered all along its branches
From short to long, upside, down, slanted
They create strange shapes as they twist along
Giving a branch an unique shape all its own

Winter; a bleak time of the year this tree is at rest
Most of its leaves gone but a few hang on at their best
The branches are bare exposed to winter's stinging lash
Yet sturdy to weather until the events of spring will appear

Where leaves used to be, round brown spheres I see
Each sphere the size of large marble they be
On a strand of now brown stems hanging low
With sharp barbs to help its seeds be delivered below

The warmth of the days beckon oncoming spring
As the dormant life within begins to stir
Tiny buds of green begin to emerge
Breaking the cycle of the winter's long cold stroll

Finally the fullness of summer can be seem
Lush leaves of green, star shape they be
Cover the tree from branch tip to stretching top
For the beauty of creation will never be stopped

Hidden among the leaves of green
Seedpods of green begin to spring forth
In a spherical manner they slowly grow
Brown tipped, spiked, speckled green and white we know

Cooler winds and lowering light rustle its leaves
For summer is beginning to waive
As the coolness of autumn's days begin to emerge
Autumn will paint the leaves, which is now forth coming

Some trees change leaves, but one color for sure
Yellow, red, brown or orange are all to adore
Yet this wondrous tree displays its autumn's wears
From midnight black to a pale green hue leaves appear

The beauty of this tree can only be seen
In the fall of the year far from the spring scene
Its beauty of colors dwarfs all others around
Bring color to the world, as the countryside slowly turns brown

I thank God for the colors of autumn when it appears
A rainbow that brighten the leaves as they cling to the trees
Telling us all that the harvest is here and now
To store up for the winter coming so close and near

God gave us nature to watch and enjoy
To learn from its patterns of seasonal joy
Life goes on from spring's birth to winter's deep sleep
The circle of life we all must keep

**Thank you God for the glorious beauty You
bring to this Earth and the seasons swing**

Buzz

A Parade

I was part of a parade the other day
Yes a parade, not fancy but a parade
At my feet were palm branches
To smooth my steps, cloaks also lay in my path

As I passed by crowds gathered and cheering
Shouts of Hosanna filled the air
Each step I took was more exciting than the last
I held my head up high as I passed by

Ahead of myself I jumped too soon
Sorry I am for it was a joyful day
It all started as my master led me out
Of my stall for my morning meal

For as a beast of burden I had work to do that day
Two men came and led me away
My master said it was ok
Following those men I did not know what was in store

To a group of men they led me
Then upon my back a cloak was placed
A little warm for a spring day
Then a young man sat on my back for the very first time

He was not that heavy, as far as I could tell
Heading toward the city we did go
People began to take notice of our little parade
Shouts of Hosanna could be heard

What a joyous day as I led that parade
Cushioned were my feet on palms and cloaks
Up to the city gates we did go
And in tow were my rider's followers all aglow

When we reached the city gates, the end of the trail
He dismounted me; a friendly thank you was heard
I was then led away back
To my stall for the rest of the day

That was a joyful day for me
For a humble donkey I be
Who carried the noblest of all men
For He was said to be the King of all Kings

I know not what happened to that man
For I began carrying things the next day
For once I was a noble stead
Who carried a King, a joyful day

God uses us in many a way
Be it the humblest of objects
Or the mightiest of people and things
We are all part of God's Creation

Thank you God for using the simplest things for your Glory

Buzz

A Path

Walking in the woods one day
I crossed a path that crossed my way
Where it started or where it ended I knew not
The path was mute and did not say

I followed it a little ways
It led me through woods so green
Some branches low I had to sway
Around several bends as it led the way

A path is a journey to somewhere out there
Some are smooth and easy to see the way
Others are rocky; a challenge to transverse are they
Windy or straight they all require a certain gate

They bring us closer to the world outside
Where birds sing and soar on high
With the sweet aroma of wild flowers in bloom
And the fresh scent of fresh air does loom

Slowly go on the path that ahead
Listen and see the world around
Filled with images of wonders that be
And different sounds only the ears to please

For life is a path we must all follow
Sometimes smooth, peaceful and serene
Other times rocky with obstacles, a dreadful scene
Yet we must go on the path ahead

God gave us a path to travel
Obstacles a plenty to test our faith
With a guiding hand He helps us through
For the path of life we must pursue

The path He leads us on may have many turns
Side paths that we may see and yearn
For the best path is to follow the Son
To His eternal Home, our victory won

Thank You God for Your Son to lead us on the paths of our lives

Buzz

Proverbs 3:6 "in all thy ways acknowledge him, and he shall
direct thy path" KJV

A Road

Oh would I like to be a road
Travel far from who knows where to there
On Interstates wide and smooth to county lanes
Twisting and turning around curve after curve

Over mountain passes and down the twisting other side
Skimming over straight desert straight-a-ways
Hills, water and valleys pass quickly by
Watching the scenery pass in a blur

Two lane roads slow you down for more to see
Then comes the single lane dirt path
With holes in the path and rocks to contend
Letting us see the world in a fresh new way

Over the years things have passed on roads
Feet walked and ran many a mile
Then came horses, donkeys, chariots and wagons
Armies, travelers have all passed their way

Many of these paths have become famous
The Appian Way, Oregon Trail, Trail of Tears
All are part of the heritage and Way
Expanding the expansion of mankind to this day

As a road I would have seen many things
People of peace, people of war and people of new beginning
Marches for justice, peace, truth and dreaded war
All throughout the ages and times to come

The time, as a road, I would most enjoy and dread
Would be long ago, far away, when a person passed my way
He traveled alone and with a group of twelve or more
Miles upon foot He traveled for three years, a short time for sure

This man of peace traveled my dusty paths and roads
Teaching a Way that will last beyond today
Filling lives with a new sense of purpose and hope
To honor and trust in the Almighty God, He spoke

I dreaded that day He walked my way
Dragging Our cross up that hill far away
A one-trip to save us all
Saving us all from a dreadful fall

The road may be rocky, steep, curved or straight
Obstacles in the way or smooth and safe
For the path He trod over my many miles
Gives a Way to travel for us and the road ahead

Oh would I like to be a road
To feel the feet of that man of peace
And cushion His feet as He spread the Word
And the others who followed His path onward

Thank you God for a path to follow

Buzz

A Seed

Walking outside the other day
No particular place did I venture to stray
But when I got back to the place I reside
My socks were coated with burs on both sides

But what are these burs I wanted to know
An irritation to my socks so low
Picking them off I realized what they were
Seeds, I had moved from somewhere to here

Looking around I saw seeds abound
The pod of the iris was open and most of the seeds gone
A pine cone there on the dusty ground
Then an acorn hit the ground with a plunking sound

Seeds all around that make the world grow
Green and fruitful as we all know
Providing us with food and such
A bounty far more than enough

But then I remembered a seed planted long ago
It has grown from a small group you know
To stretch around the world it does
With its message that God is forgiveness and Love

Christ started the seed that has flourished for many a year
Growing and nourishing as it enter the ear
Leading us forward all the Way
To a glorious return of our Savior some day

Thank You God for Your Son who sow the seed

Buzz

Comments from a reader

"It made me ponder the seed that God implanted in each of his creation."

"Jesus' seed is our example of bringing God energy into everything."

"What about the seed God planted in me?

"Have I allowed that to sprout, grow, be nurtured in order to have flower and spread God's seed?

Am I a seed and if so have I produced seeds?

A Shepherd Boy

What a night, What a night

That night the stars so bright
So bright it seemed I could tough the light
The night breeze was a little cold
For I am a shepherd but; 12 years old

My master has me do the night watch
With several other shepherds, we tend the flock
Watching the flock to keep them out of danger
Making sure we have no unexpected stranger

Peaceful and quiet the night be
As we watch the sleeping sheep, we see
In the distance we can see a town's lights
And above a clear night, stars so bright

From a distance voices could be heard
Louder and louder we could hear words
Strange to be heard, way out here
Rather scary sounds came to our ears

Then they came into view
People with wings singing as they did appear
I was shaking in great fear
They told of a birth of a Savior King in the town near

We had heard of prophets of old
Telling of a Savior to come as the story is told
Who would restore our land so grand
Again to be the promise land

They told us where the baby would be
In a manger in a cave we could see
Some of them left in glorious song
Praise God that wondrous night long

Should we go or should we stay
To see the Savoir in a manger lays
I was reluctant to go that way
Yet we felt it would be ok

So down to the town without delay
To see our Savior they said in a manger lays
We found the cave on the outskirts of town
Guided by the Angelic sound

There he was in a manger, he did lay
A beautiful yet humble display
Surrounded by his mother and father dear
In this little cave oxen and two donkeys stood near

We stayed just a little while
Marveling at what we had heard and just seen
For it is not every day you see a baby Savior King
For we have just witnessed a most marvelous thing

Saying good bye to the family we went on our way
Back to the hills not that far away
Speaking to each other of the sight we had seen
And thanking God for inviting us to that scene

Angels came telling us of a Savior just born
In a cave humble so forlorn
We saw the prophet's word come true
A Savior King for me and you

What a night, What a night

Thank You for the shepherd's story and the night of glory

Buzz

A Special night Donkey, Ox and Friends

Setting: Long time ago in a cave.

(Ox)   What is all that commotion in town? People everywhere from all over including soldiers. The town's folk are complaining. Why a census at this time? What is a census any way?

(Donkey)   A census is to counting all the people. Well you know the government; always wanting to be in control. Just wait a couple of days and we will be back to normal. You pull the cart and me carrying the wood. Time to get some rest.

(o)   Yes bossy. Oh some nice warm straw for a bed in a nice warm cave.

(d)   Finally she is quiet

(o)   I heard that.

(d)   What is that in the distance? Is it coming this way? Looks like a donkey and people.

(o)   I hope they don't come this way and stay. Donkeys snore.

(d)   With two people. A young woman and a man leading the donkey. By the way you do snore.

(o)   I sure hope they just pass by.

(d)   Quit complaining and relax.

(o)	Well here they come. They are going to stop. Why this place? I am nice and comfortable. We will have to get up and greet them. What is wrong with that lady, with the big belly?
(d)	She is going to have a baby.
(o)	Here?
(d)	Don't know maybe.
(o)	Not in my cave.
(d)	Your cave? Our cave. And I say if that be the case that the case.
(o)	Babies make me nervous. They cry and cry.
(d)	Do not worry it will not be for long. Morning is not that far away.
(o)	"Well hello donkey I am Bossy the oxen and this is David the donkey."
(d2)	They call me Jesse and I carry my master's wife Mary from Nazareth here for the census. She is with child and there was no room in town. So an innkeeper says we could stay here. Oh my master's name is Joseph.
(d)	Well come on in and get comfortable. When is the baby due?
(d2)	Any time now. Mind if I curl up in the corner? I feel tired; it has been a long day.
(o)	Be our guest. Fresh hay in the back.
(o)	Where is the man going?
(d)	I think to get some help, for I think it is time for the baby.
(o)	She sounds as if she is in terrible pain.
(d)	Here comes the man and another lady.
(d2)	My master has returning, I believe the lady is a midwife.
(o)	Will she be ok? I sure hope so.
	It is a boy

(d)	Calm down, now take a deep breath I know you get nervous around babies.
(o)	But they are placing him in our feeding trough. What are we to do now?
(d)	We will be ok, don't worry.
(o)	What is that light and who are those people with wings?
(d)	People with wings. You are seeing things.
(o)	Look for yourself. See I told you so.
(d)	Is that singing I hear? There is something very special about this couple and baby. Something very special.
(o)	He sure is quiet.
(d)	I think I hear something else other than the singing!
(o)	I hope it is not more people. It is crowded enough in here. What or who it is, it is getting closer.
(d)	Shepards and sheep. I can see them coming this way.
(o)	I do not like sheep.
(d)	For what reason?
(o)	Well they are small, bleat a lot and do not do any work.
(d)	Maybe they came to see the baby. I told you the baby boy is special.
	Miss sheep why are you here?
(s)	Well you will not believe this but a bright light filled the night sky. We heard human voices singing. The shepards were told of a special event. So we followed the shepards and here we are. You do not believe me do you?
(d)	Yes we do for we heard similar voices when the baby was born. Well get comfortable and go see the baby.
(s)	Thank you. What a beautiful baby. He is so quiet.

(o)   So much for a peaceful night. We have a couple with a new baby and their donkey, sheep and their shepards, and the baby in our feed trough. Oh then voices when the baby we born. What next, camels? Maybe when the sun comes up some peace and quiet. We will be back at work.

(d)   Peace and quiet may be but as you said back to work. Try and get some rest.

(o)   That was one sleepless special night. It is not every night a baby is born in our cave. Jesse what is going to happen now?

(d2)   I am not too sure. My master has to go to town for the census then maybe back to Nazareth, do not know.

(o)   Have a good trip and take care of the baby.

(d)   We have to go to work.

       The couple left later in the day. We were told after we got back from work.

       (A few days later.)

(o)   You will never guess who I saw the today as I was pulling my cart. I saw Jesse the donkey. He told me that his master found work here in the town and they would not be returning to Nazareth. Jesse also said that mother and baby were doing fine.

(d)   Thank you for letting me guess. Oh and thank you for letting me know.

       (A year and a half later)

(o)   Donkey, remember my broken yoke.

(d)   That just happened yesterday.

(o)   Our master took me to a carpenter. He was the same man who came to our cave. He made me a new yoke. That baby, now a toddler, was running around and playing and having lots of fun. Seeing him and his mother brought back memories of that special night and his birth.

(d)   I was wondering what happen to that couple and special child. They are still in town you say? Now that you mentioned them the memories of that night are special. I sure hope they have a special life. Time to get some rest, good night Bossy.

(o)   Good night David.

Buzz

Almost A Spring Day

Winter is almost gone for the snow has passed away
Winter hangs on yet Spring is almost here
It could happen most any day
For the winds are warmer and sun is higher on display

Brown leaves still cling to the trees
As they wait for warmer times to be pushed aside
Some green does appear on the ground below
For the stems of some flower so slightly are beginning to grow

The rain when it comes is warmer these days
Wetting the ground in a nourishing display
The sun awakening the ground as it rises overhead
Warming the land with the seeds ready to spread

For Spring is coming near
When will the first robin appear
To usher in the blossoming days of Spring
And let Winter's cold be a passing thing

The Lord God created this wondrous scene
To remind us of new birth, resurrection and greening of things
Of new beginnings and a fresh start
For Spring will soon be here along with the meadow lark

**Thank you God for the newness and
anticipation of the upcoming Spring**

Buzz

A Spring Rain

A Spring rain came the other day
Not with booming thunder on display
But a gentle rain that came from the sky
Wetting the land and plants from on high

It did not come with an ominous dark sky
With gray clouds slowly moving on by
A change could be felt as the humidity did rise
Cooling the air, coloring the sky

The rain did not come with a burst from the sky
But slowly and gently it came from on high
Gently it was tapping on the roof above
Filling the gutters with its liquid love

Outside I did venture to feel the rain
Warm to the touch, I did not complain
Gently it fell on my face and the grass
Refreshing the air, I wish it could last

The light brown ground had turned darker this day
For the rain has chased the dust away
On the leaves, droplets are making the leaves droop down
For soon the droplets will soon fall to the ground

All around the rain has cleaned the land and air
Bringing life giving water to nurture ever where
Life giving water has fallen from on high
Nourishing the land from the clouds in the sky

Like the water from on high
The life giving water from our Savior divine
Cleanses the mind and soul
Bringing us closer to God and the Spirit, making us whole

Thank You God for the rain and the living water from on high

Buzz

Summer Night

A summer night is an event to behold
It comes after the sun has passed below the horizon
Some days it quickly appears
Other times the summer dusk lingers

Summer heat has passed to the warmth of the early evening
Light is quickly fading as the lights of night
Begin to appears in the darkening canopy above
Slowly then more quickly small lights fill the sky

As they light the evening sky
They soften the darkness with their twinkling lights
Creating patterns in the night sky
Many a figures can be seen on high

The summer moon has its mystic warmth
Casting its borrowed light to enlight the scene
On occasion a cloud passes by
Taking and spreading out the light of the moon

The sounds of the day have faded away
For they have been replaced by the crickets song
Filling the air with their beckoning call
For here I am, try to find me tonight

Fireflies are not where I now live
But I have seen them in the evening darkness
Flickering and flashing on the branches they be
Creating spectacles of lights not far from me

Many things happen in the darkness of the night
Unseen are the wonders of the darkness
The day creatures are at rest, night creatures are moving
Unseen doing their nightly duties before the morning light

For the summer night is as wonderful as the day
An event only God could create
A harmony exists between the day and night
Refreshing as the night moves on

God has touched the night with His blessings
Coolness, calming, and peaceful rest from the day
Preparing us for a new day's adventure
Into the Light and Way we are to partake

Thank You God for the beauty of the night

Buzz

A Thorn Bush

I may be called a bush or jujube-tree
A plant that seems to be of no value, but goats like me
Growing in most every dry place I be
Surviving on little water, strong and free

My branches are strong and long you see
With thorns like spikes to protect me
Sharp are my tips like needles long
For I am cursed by many as they sometimes touch my thorns

Hearing a commotion I wonder what's happening
Soldiers leading a man to another man then a sentence be
The convicted they said was a King of all Jews
He looked not like a king in a cloak so common, not new

A soldier came over to me and cut some branches
Weaving them in and out he formed a circle
My thorns pierced his hands as another branch he entwined
Then he placed the wreath on the head of the King

I could feel His pain as I was placed on His head
My thorns broke His skin as His blood did flow
Down His face to the ground below
For I had become a crown of thorns that day

He wore me during the morning light
Then through the streets of Jerusalem at the crowds delight
I again could feel His pain although I tried to ease His pain
Then up to the hill to the place they called the Skull

This man then was crucified on a cross of wood He bore
I was discarded, as was His robe that day
Forgotten again, a pile of thorns thrown away
For once I was a crown on an innocent man

I regret the pain inflicted that day
On the head of an innocent man of peace they say
I had touched His life for a brief period of time
For I was a humble crown on the King of us all

**Thank You God for Your Son who lovingly
wore the crown of thorns for us all**

Buzz

A Tool Box

A tool box holds many tools, you see
Boxes varies in size, very large, or small they can be
Providing a tool for what every you may need
To do the job with, much more speed

Many a profession, or not, has a tool box near by
Be it doctor, carpenter, accountant, or pilot in the sky
All with the right tool to accomplish the job
Be it wrench, computer, manual, or saw to cut a log

As we go about our way each and every day
We use many of our own, tool boxes on the way
Pulling out the tool we may need
Fulfilling the need at times with great; sometimes speed

Yet the tool box that is for me; really dear
Is the tool box that has been, with me for many a year
It carries all the tools I need, for any situation that may arise
For within its box, a manual, are answers,
to problems anyone may devise

This manual, tool box, was written over several years
Edited by many contributors, some living in fear
Compiled and translated to language I understand
Chapter and verse it guides, me through the task at hand

This tool box is the Bible you see
That happens to be, a moral compass for me
Telling me the way I should conduct myself
And filling me with God's, untold love and wealth

Thank You God for Your tool box, the Bible, and its guidance

Buzz

A Walk

Walking outside the other day
I came across a wondrous display
At first it was hard to hear
For the world of man was in my ear

The sounds of man were still around
Yet it began to slowly fade away
Softly at first then closer the sounds came
Filling my ears with something familiar yet strange

At first it was a single sound
That grew into a song quite resound
It grew as all melodies must do
More and more the sound of man did disappear too

Other voices I came to hear
Adding their voices coming nearer
They sang their own song now loud and clear
A harmony that was pleasing to the ear

From many directions the songs did appear
Some close and near other faint to the ear
The songs of nature; man sounds make them harder to hear
For they come when you are quiet and open your ears

For the songs of nature are beautiful wondrous music
Only to be heard if we take the time
To listen away from the sounds of man
A symphony in beautiful harmony

Listen to the wind as it moves the leaves
The babbling of the brook as it slides to the sea
Waves as they splash on the rocky shore
Songs of the birds as they fly and soar

All of these and many more
Are here for us to see, hear and enjoy
Take the time to listen and see
The wonders of God's creativity

Thank You God for the sounds and sights of Your creation

Buzz

A Wedding

A special event happened the other day
Two became one in a lovely display
The ceremony was unique in its own special way
Filling the church with love in abundant array

A man (   ) and a woman (   ) were united as one
To spend their lives under the guidance of the Son
Traveling a new road that can be smooth and rough
With many hills and valleys, at times very tough

For joy is there in the love they profess
To be nurtured as time will progress
A bond that is born to stay
New adventures for them both on their way

The love they share is shared above
For God has blessed this couple in love
To cherish each moment they do share
In God we Trust will have a hand in their care

Thank You God for blessing the marriage of (   ) and (   ) forever

Buzz

A Weed

A weed an obnoxious plant
That grows in a place we do not want
Sprouting its leaves and thorns as it grows high
Spoiling the green grass of its carpet so green it does lie

Convention says no weeds there should be
To spoil the scene of beauty to see
Conformity and harmony the world must be
No weeds around for us to see

But let us take another look-see
Do we really want conformity
It is the easy path to follow, you see
Down the lazy path to mediocrity

Thank God for those who are weeds
They break the norm and set themselves and us free
Free to grow on a different yet wider path
They actually improve our lives over the past

There are many people through centuries passed
Who helped us form a new and better path
They drew their strength from one long ago
Who died on a cross to save our sinful soul

He came to earth a baby so small
And grew to be a man, we know not how tall
A thorn in the side of the religious rulers of old
A weed that must be removed, way too bold

But this weed of a man was trouble you see
His message blossomed indeed too many weeds
Who spread a new Way from sea to sea
That has changed the landscape and mindset for you and me

God gave His Son, a weed He be
For us to follow and be like Him
To reach out of the norm
To follow His Way, a weed like He

Thank You God for your Son, may I be a weed like He

Buzz

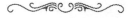

A Whisper

Words heard in a quiet mode
Usually between you and me
Telling a secret or words of love
Of importance they always be

But those are not all the whispers I hear
Coming to me upon my ear
Messages soft and clear
Of the world we live in far and near

Nature does whispers all the time
Like the gentle breeze rustles in the pines
Tell us to look at nature as His grand design
The beauty we so feebly try to define

The leaves that rustles in the woods
A deer being as stealthful as it could
The trickle of a mountain stream
The flight of a butterfly on wing, so keen

All whispers and more of the world from a Creator Great
That wants us to see nature in its pure state
A world He created for you and me
To listen and enjoy, a special blessing it be

Thank You God for letting us hear the whispers of Your creation

Buzz

Wind Chime

A wind chime hangs outside my door
Silent now for the breeze is no more
It waits for the breeze to move its chimes
And bring sweet sounds to the world so divine

Wind chimes come in many sizes and designs
Short too long, all are musical and very fine
The larger one, deep with tone
While the short ones are higher in pitch, hardly alone

The middle size ones have music each of their own
Not to deep or shrill but between with beautiful tones
The ones I enjoy are the chimes, long and wide
That product a sound for me, low and mellow that moves my insides

The Holy Spirit is like a wind chime
Entering a person, beautiful music in the making, so divine
Filling us with the glory and the love of God
For His love, benevolence and forgiveness we give Him laud

Music to the soul, the Holy Spirit be
A new life to behold, you will see
Lighting the way to a new adventures, be it land or sea
For the soul is now cleansed of it sinful passed, a new future it will be

**Thank You God for the Holy Spirit, like the
wind chime, new music to the soul**

Buzz

Abandoned

Am I forgotten
Has life past me by
Am I worthless and of little value
Where have they all gone

We think of someone abandoned at sea
Left alone far away from where anyone be
Isolated without a soul around
Wondering if you would ever be found

The first day of school a traumatic event
Wondering where your parents went
Left along to fend for your self
You would like to hide in a corner or on a shelf

The first day at a new job
You feel abandoned yet in a mob
In an alien place
Looking and looking for a friendly face

Then comes the first day a person retires
After a long time working, rest you desire
Where has the entire fellow workers gone
For I feel abandoned for they work on

Many women and men felt alone in Bible times
Feeling abandon by God they thought was by design
Only to realize that God was by their side
Strengthen them for the next new adventure ride

Yet we may feel abandoned from time to time
We only need to look to the power divine
For there no matter how abandoned we may feel
God is always nearby, for you and me, a real big deal

Thank You God for I know you are always near

Buzz

Advent has Arrived

Once again this time of year, Advent is here
It came very quickly this year
For just the other day Fall did appear
And now we have Advent here

A time to reflect on the year passed
And the Christmas story that comes at last
For Advent is here and my soul rejoices
Of the telling of the story of love and the Angelic Voices

Candles are lit to tell the story
Of a birth long ago that came in humble glory
Candles of pink, purple and white they be
Lighting the world with love, joy, hope and peace for you and me

A single candle light breaks the darkness
Bringing a new light and hope to the world needing niceness
Slowly warming the cold heart
For a new day is coming as darkness departs

Then a second breaks the gloomy day
Giving us more light to pass our way
An inner peace does fill me
For lasting peace has come for now I see

A third candle shows more light
Moving the darkness further out of sight
For the love of Mary brought forth a son
That the world of darkness will soon be done

Still more light from the candle four
For now we have an open door
As joy abounds in the story foretold
Of a Savior born so long ago in days of old

There is but one more candle so bright
The center one the color white
Its brightness tells of love and sacrifice
For the Son of God Most High is the True Light

For Advent is a time to rejoice
A time to remember those Angelic Voices
Proclaiming the birth of a baby boy long ago
Who would go on to save our sinful souls

Thank You God for Your son we call Emmanuel

Buzz

Advent

The season of Advent is upon us now
It comes shortly after the Thanksgiving and the end of Fall
A time to prepare for a much anticipated event
We have heard told many times before

Its symbol is an unique display
Of five candles all set in a wreath array
One of pink and three of purple form a ring
With one white candle in the middle of them all

One candle is lit for each week that comes
Each to glow for thoughts to ponder
All building to a climax of an event to come
Lighting and warming the darkness for a blessed Son

A purple candle is lit, the first to begin
Of *Hope*, to show and prepare the highway
Of prophesies long ago of Him to come
To ease our path along our Way

A second purple candle following the first
Of *Peace* to come here and for me
To clear the mind of troubling events
And calm my own turbulent sea

A third purple candle to follow the two
Of *Love* that will come to me and you
From a person we long to be
For He's the One who shepherds we

Pink is the candle that follows the purple three
Of *Joy* for me from now to eternity
A gift that no money can buy,
Warming the soul to an everlasting high

Yet there is one left to be lit on a special day
That of the central white candle on display
A representation of the one who comes
The boy child of Mary, God's only begotten Son

Thank You God for Advent and it's time to reflect

Buzz

After the event

The grand anticipation has passed
Good cheer and glad tiding have faded
The day of Christmas has become a memory once more
Pre-season normality has reluctantly returned

The tree is now void of its brightly wrapped boxes
The routine of days is quickly returning
For our attention is now on the coming New Year
The world continues as if that special day had not occurred

But back we must go and we should staystay
To the event of that night so long ago and far away
Ceramic figures tell of that night long ago
That changed the darkness into bright light like sunlight on snow

The crèche has become a mute little display
Yet each figure says volumes in its own way
Of adventures in the past and of adventures to come
We know each story by heart but love to hear them again and again

Shepherds who saw the heavenly host
A donkey that carried the mother who gave birth
A stable filled with animals and hay
A star that led Wise Men on their way

They need not let fade these memories away
The ceramic figures should remind us day after day
Of the Best Gift we received on that glorious event
God's Love will never be forgotten

Thank You God for the crèche and its eternal story

Buzz

Alternate Beginning (Time in Denver)

The time of anticipation has passed
The excitement has passed and we return
To the time we have weeks before
Back to the routine of the time past forth

The wrapping all strung around the floor
Are all bundled up and recycled to outdoors
The tree still stands yet the luster is gone
For the day of anticipation is now bygone

Alone in Silence

Alone I sit in silence
Hearing but the clock as it passes time
Occasionally a small drip will hit the sink
Then silence again except for a tick

Looking around the room at what is there
Memories of things I did share
That touched many lives now and then
Items that I do share and care for

In silence the memories come slow and sure
A picture sits alone on a stand
Telling of times passed and gone
In a frame that is gold leaf all around

Looking again I see another picture, another friend
Alone I remember the times we shared
The picture of my grandchild so alive and bright
Filling my mind with a special light

Silence continues except for the clock
Passing its time with a tick and a tock
A book I have spotted on a shelf close at hand
With frayed edges like a elegant fan

The silence is broken with the rustling of the pages
For this book speaks in loud clear phrases
From the people who are on the inside
Telling of the silence and loneliness they endured

The book tells of a man named Jonah at sea
Running away from a job given to he
Cast into the sea now alone he might be
Silence in the belly of the beast at sea

Pages turn and another appears
A queen in a foreign land not her's
Alone in her convictions she challenges a man
In silence she makes her ultimate stand

In a prison cell he sat alone
Speaking his mind to a king on a throne
Silence was his companion in his prison cell
Knowing the truth of what he did say so well

In silence He walked to a garden that night
Alone with His friends and prayers He did speak
To pray for guidance to His Father above
Only to be taken away to a judge

All these people were alone in some way
In silence did they pray
To do the right thing for the people they loved
For they all got guidance from above

We may feel alone in silence any day
But that book on the table has something to say
In silence there are words to be heard
Words that you are worthy and a child of the Almighty God

God is with us day after day
Listening to those alone who sit in silence
Alone we may feel yet God is always nearby
To take away our loneliness and silent our fears

Thank You God for speaking to us in our lonely silence

Buzz

Alone

Alone I sit in my easy chair
Wondering why this may be
My companion is gone away from me you can see
To work, play, outside stuff or Heaven, but not with me

Sitting here I wonder what to do
For the house is empty especially without you
There are always things I can do
Read, study, housework; to mention a few

As I sit and think of being alone
I think of those who are alone like me
Jonah in the midst of the sea
Jesus in the Garden of Gethsemane

John in exile scribed to a church afar
Joseph, David, Esther, Ruth, or Mary
All and more were alone like me
Yet I began to read more of all those who are

I found that God was with them all the way
Filling them with life and love divine
Showing them all they were not alone
But safe in the thoughts and arms of a Loving God

My companion may be gone; not far away
For my memories will with me stay
And I know that God is here this day
To comfort and guide my daily way

Thank you God for your comfort when I am alone

Buzz

An Apple

"An apple a day keeps the doctor away"
That is what the folk lore say
A nutritious fruit what fits the bill
At least it does not come in a pill

They come in shapes, mostly round
In many colors even a light brown
Mainly in shades of red they be
At harvest time they are plentiful on the tree

They start out as tiny flowers that blooms in the spring
Attracting the bees who do their thing
Taking nourishment from the tree on which they belong
Growing and growing in the summer sun so long

When autumn comes they are full in size
Red, ripe and beautiful to the eyes
Ready, for the harvest near
Very tempting to the local deer

We as followers are like that apple you see
For Jesus is like that apple tree
Giving us new life and forgiving our sins
Nourished by His words we thrive and win

For we are the fruit of His word
Bringing action and meaning to what we have heard
Loving those who our are enemies and friends
Praising the Lord to the very end

An apple we be
From God's living Son, the apple tree
For with His help evil we will defeat
And following His example is really neat

Thank You God for Your Son our giver of life

Buzz

An Invisible Force

The wind, the breeze where do you go
You start somewhere, I do not know
Moving across the land, some time fast other times slow
I can see where you have been but where you go, I do not know

Your names are many from land to land
I sure wish I could hold you in my hand
The sea moves at your command
Waves high and low crash on rock and sand

You move the clouds high above
Creating figures of things like a dove
Or creatures fierce as can be
Then they fade away on a sky blue sea

Storms you have brought from far away
Dark clouds with hail or rain on the way
And in the cold months the snow may fall
Piling the white snow up against a wall

As summer breezes blow, they are a delightful thing
Light and warm they move the windsock with a gentle swing
Rustling the grass and leaves on high
You even help the birds to soar and fly

But the wind that captures my thoughts
Are the divine winds that God has brought
That fills my mind and soul with wonders so bold
Of the Spirit of God that has entered my soul

The winds of God, the Holy Spirit it be
Fills my being with His love for me
Guiding me through life day to day
Helping me see the world in a brand new Way

**Thank You God for Your Spirit, like the
wind, that guides me day by day**

Buzz

An Umbrella

The umbrella an interest mechanical device
One of the things it does is protect us from the light
And on other occasions from the wind and rain
When folded down it becomes a cane

Its comes in sizes, great and small
One on a drink glass, pretty paper and tall
Brightly colored with designs many and unique
Others that causes me, to think of sleep

One I saw that advertized someone wears
Many I saw during the sunny fair
Held up by an up stretched hand
With its top, a very colorful triangular set of bands

Some umbrella handles are quite ornate
Carved, shaped in intricate designs, people can decorate
Others on long poles in a sturdy stand
Underneath we can eat a meal with our toes in the sand

Yet the umbrella I like has no handle or cloth
It protects me, an awful lot
When I need help it is always there
For God my umbrella, He is everywhere

When sorrow deep, He is there for me and you
Being a protector and comforter, true blue
Easing the pain, taking the sin away
Leading us on a different, new glorious Way

Thank you God for Your umbrella of protect and comfort

Buzz

An Unusual Plant

Walking about the other fine day
I spotted a plant along my way
Out of place in this forest green
A desert plant hardy and not at all lean

With leaves of green long, sharp and straight
Reaching out for all to see
Spreading out to the ground and sky above
As green as green can be

In the center a stalk came forth
Towering above the plant leafy fort
And upon this stalk flowers of white
Hanging downward in the summer's warm sunlight

Flowers white as snow like fluffy clouds above
Upside down as delicate as a china cup
Six petals form this flower so white
That close to form a dew drop shape at night

They filled the stalk to the tip
Rows upon rows they reach the top
With petals wide open in the summer sun
A delight to view and oh what fun

This beautiful plant has an unusual name
It is a Yucca plant by fame
A creation for the desert lands
A beauty wherever it stands

A desert plant as you can see
A creation by the Almighty
Out of place in this forest scene
Yet growing well in a forest green

We all may be out of place at times
But in His arms we are all fine
For we can live in harmony with others
For in God's Love we are all God's children: sisters and brothers

Thank You God for those who are different as we live in harmony

Buzz

Anniversary

An Anniversary occurred the other day
A celebration of an event they do say
Of an event that happened long ago
Or maybe just a year or so

Anniversaries are like birthday
They occur but once a year
Celebrating an event some held so dear
Others we would like to forget; too near

Each Anniversary is an event that happened
An event in history some of us surely do know
An event that may be tragic or extremely a delight
Making us very happy or mad enough to fight

God gave us anniversaries we should remember
He gave us what tradition says; was in December
Another that comes at Easter time
Both of a Man that was holy and very divine

Many more we could count forth
Of days and times we treasure the most
Yet two we celebrate the most of all
Be them by ourselves or a group in a large hall

For God wants us to celebrate our miracle of birth
The days of our lives and its gifts are worth
As well as the event when man and a woman become one
Living together with the blessings of His Own Son

This celebration was of a wedding you see
That happened many years ago with me
Spanning the years with you and me
Sharing times and memories

Thank You God for the many Anniversaries you have granted us

Buzz

Baptism

Baptism is a Birthday; a wondrous day
At that time we express we will follow His Way
For on us is water a public holy displayed
As The Holy Spirit comes down to us in full array

We may be sprinkled or water surround
Young of age or mature and sound
For now we are new
With special things we must do

To follow Jesus who showed us a New Way
Loving our neighbors no matter they be
Different from the person that is me
Respecting the creation all around

It's a birthday you see
A new life of love from Him to me
For we now see the world in a different light
With the Son of Man who shines so bright

But we in Christ, should not forget our special birthday
That day we were born again to stay
In the arms of our loving God
For we accepted His Son, our guide and to follow His Way

Thank You God for Baptism as we join Your Son and the Way

Buzz

Before Christmas

For the time is coming near
An anticipated event is coming bright and clear
Filling this gloomy darkening time of year with cheer
For Christmas time is almost here

As signs appear we hold close and dear
Times that have passed and of others near
Tinsels trim and ornaments on tree and wall
Stocking on the mantle when filled hopefully will not fall

Lights that do twinkle and colors oh so warm
Wreathes on the door that welcome you home
Candles that burn a warm flickering light
And family members far and near we visit; such a delight

But why the reason of this amount of good cheer
A baby boy was born not of this year
But long ago and a place and time far away
He came to us as a gift on one glorious day

A gift, you see, from Our Father above
Of everlasting, eternal, forgiving, and wondrous Love
A baby boy who came to show us the Way
Of God's everlasting Love; day after day after day

Thank You God for the real meaning of Christmas

Buzz

Birthday

A birthday comes once a year
It tells the time we are here
To celebrate the year just passed
And to prepare for the next year that comes too fast

We may celebrate them alone or with friends
A day to forget or a celebration that does not end
Memories of birthdays we have had past
Or as a child, hoping the day will always last

As we grow older, birthdays come too fast
For we want the days to more slowly pass
To savor the time that we are here
And look forward to another year

We enjoy the presents and family praise
Sometimes we wish it would last several days
But as time must pass the day is done
For now one more year has just begun

God has given us birthdays to celebrate
To remind us that He gave us life
To do our best to be true to the Way
And celebrate life looking forward to the next glorious day

**Thank You God for letting us celebrate the
years of our life we have lived**

Buzz

Blessings

Blessings are something we all expect
We take for granted what we have
Most of us live a life of ease
Blessings come and we are will pleased

We go about our daily lives
Having dinner at ease about five
Get from here and then to there
At ease without even a care

We tend to look at the large blessing
That surrounds us day to day
Home, family, work, wealth, health
And forget about the small blessings

All around us we need to look and see
The blessing that have come to you and me
The health we have, the position we behold
The place we live, quite bold

Many blessings we have are those we often forget
The clothes we have and what we wear
Shoes we have to cover our feet
The ability to walk and run without care

We forget that we can tie our shoes
Tying that bow so it will not come loose
Use our eyes and mind to read the Words
Walk to and open the door

Thread a needle to fix an open seam
Fill a glass without spilling a drop
Putting a button in a button hole
Shaking the hand of a person we know

God our Creator has given us many gifts
We tend not to think of them as blessing
But everything we use to live from day by day
All that we are and do are God's blessings

For we are a blessing in the eyes of God
One of His many creations
Within this time and place we exist
One of His many blessings to serve His will

No matter how large or small we contribute
Be it ink on paper or helping other
Even if we feel down and out
We are a blessing from our Father

Thank You God for the blessing big and small you have given us

Buzz

Bread

They say. Bread "is the staff of life"
Made of wheat, water, oil and leavening
Sometimes adding seasoning to make it nice
Baked, it nourishes the body as it sustains life

It comes in many shapes and sizes
Many flavors from sour to sweet
Short and broad, long and round
And at Passover thin and flat

Yet there is bread we may partake
That fills the body in an unique way
It came to us from long ago
A meal of bread and wine for the soul

It is called by several names these days
Communion, Eucharist, and The Lord's Supper they say
All to show Love, of God day to day
Served by a man who gave His all and Love

We celebrate this meal, a small portion to partake
To remember a man who gave His all
The bread His body, the wine His blood
For us to become a part of His everlasting Love

Bread "is the staff of life"
New life that comes from a simple meal
A meal that we can refuse or take
And if we partake will sustain us forevermore

**Thank You God for Your Son symbolized
by the bread and the wine**

Buzz

Care Takers

Care takers are the forgotten people you see
They are in the background for you and me
Taking care of us from time we are born
To the end of our time, so forlorn

Our first care takers were mom and dad
Begin so small I sure was glad
To feed and clothe me they did so well
Even through some lies I did tell

Throughout the years they led the way
Helping me even in my daily play
Supporting me be I near or far
Even trusting me with the car

Over the years many care takers I have seen
School, work, home and in between
Teachers, police, friends and other seen and not seen
Doing their thing to keep us safe and serene

We take on the role at times
Looking after other, following words divine
To care for those less fortunate than you
Trying all the time to follow the Golden Rule

The hardest job is caring for the ones you love
Being near or far away
For they are in your heart day after day
Remembering the other days and glorious play

I thank the greatest care giver of all
On whom I can anytime call
My Lord and Savior who cares for all
Even when I make a sinful fall

Thank You God the ultimate and glorious Care Taker

Buzz

Changing Season

It changed the other day, a passing so noted
The calendar said that the change did occur
So suddenly it came for now it is here
A new season did appear, it came this year

I speak of Fall or Autumn; is now here
So gradually the change I forgot to see
Little by little it caught up to me
For now I do see that Fall is here to see

At first I did not see the change in green
It was darker in the summer now a paling color scene
Now as the days pass more and more green is gone
Giving way to a color pallet of orange, yellow, red and beyond

For Fall is a season of color you see
The green is gone from the great oak tree
Aspens shed their quaking yellow leaves
As a multitude of colors repaint the once green scene

Beneath the leaves, once the color of green
Are the colors of the Autumn scene
Glorious colors of red, yellow, orange and brown
Colors only a master artist can create and compound

Sunlight comes later in the morning now
And exits early in the evening hours
A little chill in the morning and evening times
Tell me that summer has passed away and gone

The sounds of the season are different to the ear
As the leaves are rustled by the cooler Fall breeze
On high is the honking of a passing flight
As migrating Canada geese head to their southern delight

For we are in a season of change
Slowly it approaches then fully emerges in glorious splendor
Telling us to prepare for the harvest is near
A time to prepare for winter's blast, no fear

God gave us this season to remember to prepare
To prepare for the times of winter's lean
In the times when the harvest is full
And the bounty of the seeds have been fulfilled

We prepare for the times of winter's lean
While living a life under the Son's loving scene
Sharing in times of plenty with those in need
Trying to live a life of love indeed

**Thank you God for the season of Fall and
time of harvesting and preparation**

Buzz

Children, Little People

Children are little people we see
Most live in a world of fantasy
Their lives are filled with times of fun
And generally they are always on the run

Children are little people you see
Enjoying the world without a care
They love to play and run all day
And learn to follow in their parents' way

We as big people need to realize
Those children have a lesson inside
To enjoy the world as we see it today
A place created just for us to stay

God gave us little people so that we may see
A world created by God for thee
To enjoy as children do, as a child of God
Living in the arms of God's everlasting Love

Thank You God for little people to show us the Way

Buzz

Christmas Carols

Tis the season, Christmas is near, rejoice
Raise your songs in humble voice
To sing the songs of new and old
We sing them soft and bold

Some are from times past
And most have been around and last
Bring memories and stories of old
Filling the air with songs that warms the soul

They tell of a time, a long time ago
Of a birth of an infant boy in a place so well we know
Of a humble birth of a very special king
That was foretold and declared on angels wings

Words bring color to the songs
The star's tail white, bright and long
Hay in a manger, yellow, where the babe does lie
A rose; red in bloom on display

The night black, dotted with starry lights
Angels wings, white glowing bright
A crown of gold for a new born king
A donkey gray watching every thing

Carols tell a story, old and new
Of a love that is always true
For unto you is born in the silent of the night
A new Way that will shine ever so bright

Thank You God for those Christmas Carols that tell of your Love

Buzz

Christmas Lights

Christmas lights are a wonderful sight
They brighten the day as well as the night
Shinning forth in a myriad of displays
Pointing towards the reason for the day

Many a color they come, to make the displays
Mainly red, green, clear and blue; they brighten the way
They light the stars, garlands and even trees
That warms the soul that is meant for you and me

So why the lights on those Christmas displays
They light the path and lead the way
To a time and miracle that happened long ago
In a place, by song, we all know

The first Christmas lights came as Angels bright
Telling the shepherds of a king born that night
The new born king to be a new light to all
Saving us all from a sinful fall

A Christmas light led the Wise Men on their way
As they traveled from the east, many a day
Bringing gifts to a child humble in birth
For God's Son had come to Earth

Christmas lights are for us to enjoy
To draw us to mentally employ
The meaning of a night with a special light
That brought God's love, as a child, into our sight

**Thank You God for Christmas light and your
Son the Way, the Truth and the Light**

Buzz

Christmas Decorations

We brought out our Christmas decorations the other day
In anticipation to set them up as a nice display
Boxes upon boxes we had to tow
Filled with decorations that almost overflowed

Unloading the boxes we found a miniature lighted town
Placing it upon a ledge on a blanket of fluffy white snow
Overlooking a frozen plastic pond with skaters three and a dog
A church, Bakery, Toy Store, school plus several more

The tree is standing tall as can be
Covered with lights of many colors so bright
Ornaments hang all over its branches so green
Of many styles and shapes they do please

Some are new and others old with memories so
Of Christmases past of friends we know
Ornaments from lands far away
Topped by a star flickering so bright

Banners and stockings decorate the walls
Garland is strung over the door so tall
Another piece over the entrance to the hall
Blinking brightly in colors of red, blue and green

Music was turned on with Christmas songs to hear
Filling the air with those traditional children's tunes
Of Rudolph and Santa and a sleigh filled with toys
Making their deliveries on Christmas Eve night without delay

Then came a song that brought me around
"Lo, how a rose e're blooming" what a sound
Where was it, it has to be here in this box of Christmas gear
And there it was that Nativity scene now near

I removed the scene with care from that box
Unpacked it on the table as careful as could be
A donkey, sheep, and cow were all there
Wise men three and a Shephard or two

The wise man came a little late to the place
For two years later they came on scene
So we set them as they came from afar
To Bethlehem still following that star

Mary and Joseph but where was the baby
Digging around in the stable I found it
Something small wrapped in tissue secure
A small manger with a baby inside

I found a place of honor to display my find
That scene I had just unwrapped
Realizing that the decorations I had set-up before
Were family traditions yet nothing more than a display

The babe in the manger is what Christmas is all about
God sent His Son to teach us a new Way
To love one another as He Loves us day after day
And forgive us of our many sins and diseases as we follow His Way

Lord God Thank You for Your Son our New Beginning

Buzz

Crescent Moon

Venturing outside in the late afternoon
Looking skyward I spotted a crescent moon
Hanging motionless in the blue sky
From where I stood it did look quite high

As the sun slowly set in the west
And the daylight got less and less
The moon began to increase its glow
As it was seen from far below

Brighter and brighter as the dusk of night came this way
Telling all creatures this is the end of another day
Night creatures began to stir from their rest
As day creatures head to their nest

A day or two later I went to view
The crescent moon in the sky so blue
The crescent moon was on longer there
But a different shape was high in the air

The crescent moon was gone, it had left the scene
Now a half moon was clearly seen
Filling the sky and brighter still
Floating high above the distant hills

For now the moon rules the early evening sky
Before the stars come up on high
Spreading its light for all to see
A guiding light for you and me

God's Son is like the phases of the moon
Using His light to remove the gloom
Bringing light onto the wages of sin
For following the Way we can win

For God sent His Son to lighten our Way
Filling the night and even the day
With the light of truth and forgiveness here to stay
Guiding us through the perils, day by day

**Thank You God for the light, be it crescent
moon, Your Love and Son**

Buzz

Darkness

Darkness comes once each day
Taking the sunlight far away
Painting the night dark and black
We wonder how long the night will last

The seasons change its length of night
In summer the darkness is shorter, what a delight
While winter darkness stays too long
As we wish of spring and its sweet song

Yet darkness gives us time to rest
When we must go to rest in our own nest
Safe from the cold and darkness of night
Waking safely in the morning light

Darkness can come in many a form
In a time when we are troubled and forlorn
With the passing of a friend
Whom we will cherish beyond the end

Darkness can come in the depth of pain
Making us depressed and down a darker lane
Or feeling like no one does care
Thinking our life is beyond repair

Yet like the night with the moon in the sky
Light there above does shine so high
For the moon is but the reflection of the sun
Bringing light to the night even though the day is done

For the sins we hold are the darkness we hold
Some may be little, others quite bold
Keeping us away from the light
Making us feel that all is not right

The darkness can be broken
With thoughts and words are spoken
When we follow a man, Royal and Divine
Out of the darkness into a world of His design

For the Son of God is the Way
To leave the darkness and live day by day
Within the brightness of the Son
The darkness and gloom are forever done

Thank you God for removing the darkness through Your Son

Buzz

Dawn

A new day has just begun
For the pale light of morning has arrived
Slowly yet steadily removing the stars
From the once darkness of the night sky

The coolness of the morning will soon pass away
As the sun creeps over the horizon
Suddenly filling the land with its golden light
Pushing the night over the far horizon

For a new day has begun
As the birds herald its coming
Raising their voices one by one
Praising the light of a new and wondrous day

The calm, serenity of the morning will fade away
For the bustle of the day will soon commence
Flowers will slowly open their petals
As the warmth of the day surrounds them

The night creatures have long retired
As the day creatures stretch their legs and wings
Challenging the new day once again
As they praising God in their own special way

For the morning is the new beginning
Of the next adventure we will encounter
A new day to enjoy the creation of God
And praise Him for all we have received

The dawn I see reminds me of the Son of God
Bringing new life and vision to mankind
Breaking us out of the darkness of sin
Providing Light and Guidance to the new Way ahead

**Thank You God for the dawn, Your Son
and a new Light to follow the Way**

Buzz

Decoration Day now Memorial Day

Memorial Day a day to remember
Those lives that were lost in wars past
From the battles of our Revolution to
The conflicts of today their memories will last

They fought and died for a noble cause
To rid the world of tyrants large and small
Who threatened the freedom
Of those the tyrants did so oppress

We honor those who died to keep us free
To live a life we all do believe
To worship and live as we please
And live a life free from tyranny glee

The battles and wars may be long ago
Or conflicts today in the world we know
Yet they sacrificed to keep us free
For they died or were maimed for our liberty

Thank you God for those who served to keep us free

Buzz

Dew

Those morning moist droplets clinging to plants
Collecting on every stem and leaf
Nourishing its recipient as it slowly moves down
Heading with other dew drops to the ground

The dew starts in the dark of night
When coolness comes out of sight
Drawing the moisture from the air above
Down to the plants we all so love

With the morning light low on the hill
Rays of sunlight fill the morning still
Hitting the dew which reflect the light
Turning the green grass sparking bright

The field of green grass is like a starry night
Twinkling in the morning light
Slowly fading as the sun does rise
Lasting but a few moments, a sweet surprise

God did give the plants the morning dew
A nourishing drop of moisture too
Help them grow and blossom forth
Bringing beauty to God's creation here on Earth

God's dew to us is nourishing too
It comes to us in a ray of light
Straight from His Word and Son so bright
Nourishment for the human soul, eternally right

Thank You God for nourishment given to all Your creation

Buzz

Dinner

We sat down to a dinner the usual way
For it was close to the end of the day
So we talked about things we did on our way
Telling of the times that we had that day

Telling of the adventures we had that very day
The wonder we had seen on display
The good times we had
And the times that made us sad

Then it occurred to me of a dinner long ago
Of the family of men who dined on tables low
In an Upper room in a land far away
In the midst of a Religious Holiday

Like us they probably talked about that very day
Of how they went along their way
Of all the events and sights seen on display
And the joyful times that came their way

For that was a special dinner that day
Since the Passover Meal was soon to be on display
A traditional dinner of an event long ago
Of a time Ancestors left a land we all know

This meal had a little twist
For this meal did not follow the usual list
The Leader washed their dusty feet
And a new pray was said short, precise and sweet

A new tradition of remembrance was started that day
The breaking of bread that stood for His body
A cup of wine to be shared by all
As a symbol of His blood He would shed

A new tradition that has been passed on
To remember that night and the sacrifice
That was made to save mankind that very day
And to follow the precepts of a new Way

We sit down to dinner most every day
Tell those around of our daily life on display
Remembering a meal and a new Way
For on that night Divine Love was here to stay

**Thank You God that we celebrate and
remember that dinner long ago**

Buzz

A Stranger on The Road

The road we trod was long that day
Both rough and smooth along that narrow way
Wheel ruts were deep and plain to see
Stretching for miles to the place we should be

We had just left the events of Jerusalem behind
Heading to the village of Emmaus, being
Witness to the death of our Rabbi, the other day
Devastated for our Rabbi was gone away

As we walked we talked about the events
The trial we heard was a sham,
Flogging was far too severe
But we heard of a new prayer He told the twelve

Rounding a corner a stranger joined our walk
He voice pleasant and we asked if he had heard the talk of the day
He said he knew not of the events of the days past
Not of our Lord who was crucified and taken away

Our destination was just over that hill as the daylight waned
The stranger was determined to go on his way
But we invited him to stay and a meal to partake
He accepted our invitation and we continued on our way

We continued to discuss the events of the past days
As a sense of calm slowly came our way
This strange told us of Moses and prophets of old
Of scriptures and what the prophets foretold

Our destination was coming into view
Entering the house we prepared for the meal
We asked him to stay at least for the meal
He said I would and a bless he must bestow

Saying the blessing and breaking the bread we suddenly
Realized this stranger we walked with was Jesus our Lord
Our sorrow was gone for our Lord was alive
He had conquered death and was risen indeed

We finished the meal and then he was gone
With haste we did return to Jerusalem to the disciples
To tell them of our news and the walk that day
Our Lord and Savior had risen, yes indeed

The walk to Emmaus may have been long ago
Where Jesus walked and calmed the soul
He is here today to do the same
As we walk with Him as we follow His Way

Thank You God for Your Son who walks with us each day

Buzz

Evening Light

The sun has set and night is coming
As dark colored paintbrush goes across the sky
Slowly changing the blue to dark of night
Dots of light appear on the canvas giving faint light

In the midst of the night a dim light appears
A spot on the horizon slowly broadens
Changing that spot and around it to shades of yellow orange
Then a beam of light crests the distant horizon

Steadily the light of night comes into view
For the light has made its début
The night-light cast it light across the sleeping land
Bringing a grayish light to those at hand

Long shadows cross the land
As trees and bushes block its rays
Yet the night-light finds its way
Through the leaves to the earth below

As the night light moves on its journey above
Shadows are ever changing on the land below
Darting in and out of the leaves as it goes
Drawing its artistic scenes as slowly it flowing by

A winter night is a beautiful sight
Reflecting off a blanket of snow so white
The night light makes the night almost bright as day
Giving the night traveler an easy way

Once again we marvel at that night-light
Waxing and waning as it passes so bright
Filling the nights with a mellow glow
Taming the night with the light we know

God has given us this night-light to glow
To lead us through the darkness we know
His Son is The Light we also need
To guide us through darkness indeed

When we follow God's Son through the darkness
The shadows will grow ever smaller
Darkness will fade away
For the Son of Man is here to stay

His Light has quelled the darkness around
Bringing Light to the troubled and sinners abound
Giving peace to mankind far and wide
As He shares His Way with you and me

God Thank You for the Light in the darkness that sets us free

Buzz

Fall is almost here
Per the calendar, it comes this time of year
With sunlight shorter
And night time being bolder

There is a coolness in the air
Sometimes I need a hat to warm my hair
A jacket to cut the morning breeze
For shortly color will come to the leaves

Now the time of harvest is near
The honk of geese going south fills my ears
Those that migrate have heard the call
For they all know that soon it will be Fall

The greens will slowly fade away
Turning to many colors on display
Filling the trees and bushes with Fall colors so bright
As the leaves quiver in the breeze and fading light

God gave us this season of harvest and change
To prepare us for Winter's chilly game
Preparing us for times and events to come
And someday the return of His Son

We harvest knowledge from His Word
Enjoying the world of nature, its sights and sounds heard
Share our harvest with our fellow man
And trying to do the best we can

Thank You God for a time to prepare for Your kingdom

Buzz

Fall is Finally Here

Fall is here; the shorter daylight hours do say
Summer has past and somewhere down the way
Winter will come some day
But Fall is here for this moment, here to stay

It has come so slowly
The calendar showed it the way
Bringing the harvest and cooler days
For a few brief months here to stay

A Fall breeze rustles the leaves as they fall to the ground
Changing the ground from green to shades of brown
For there is a chill in the morning air
And more dew is on the flora so fair

We see the trees in all their splendor
Their coats now a different color scheme we see
Showing the world a very colorful scene
Of reds, yellows, and browns with shades of lighter green

We see the creatures all prepare for the time
When winter is here and colder times will fall in line
Gathering the food they need to sustain
Or leaving this place for a climate on a far off plain

God did create this season for us to prepare
For the harvest is now we need to care
As we need to prepare for the times to come
For the Son and His Way, before time is done

Each season has its own meaning
And Fall is for gleaning
To follow the Way as set forth before
And remember to answer His knock on the door

For the season of Fall, we should always keep in mind
To prepare for the Son's harvest time
By following a path we called the Way
That leads us through even the darkest of days

Thank you God for the season of Fall and preparation

Buzz

Fire

I saw a fire the other day
With red and yellow flames dancing their own way
Filling the day with its ever glowing light
As the flames danced with abundant delight

The warmth of the fire was felt near by
As flames and smoke rose to the sky
Pieces of ash were lifted too
Up into the sky so blue

Fires can be many things
A campfire as a warming ring
A cozy cracking flame in the fireplace at home
Taking the sting off a cold winter night when home alone

Fire can be a destructive sight
Destroying a house with consuming flames and light
Or running fast in the dry grasses and trees
Creating billowing smoke bring grasses and trees to their knees

But fire can be a wonderful thing
Clearing the dead leaves for upcoming spring
Nourishing and preparing the ground for new life to begin
Cleansing the iron of the impurity within

Jesus is the fire we see
Cleansing the soul of the sin within thee
A fire of love that fills the spirit and warm the soul
Lighting the Way and making us whole

Jesus has set us Christians on fire
A fire of love and compassion is His desire
Spreading the flame of God's Holy Word
Lighting the world so that all may have heard

Thank You God for the fire of Christ Your Son

Buzz

First Buds

They have slept the long winter long
Staying protected within the branch until winter is gone
Waiting for time to come forth
Away from that winter blast from the north

The warmth of the sun on a spring day
Awaken them from their sleepy haze
Coaching them out of their winter dress
That confined them snuggly during their winter rest

For now the winter dress has opened up
As its brown coat peels away
Revealing a light green leaflets here to stay
For now we know that spring is on display

Different trees, shrubs and bushes shine
Budding forth in colors so divine
For now another spring shows its colors again
Like a rainbow of color without an end

At first their colors are not so bright
Still muted by the winter night
Yet as the warm sun does appear
More and more the colors brightness becomes so clear

Over a short time the full leaf will appear
Leaving it winter coat far in the rear
Showing its full glory to the sun above
Basking in the beauty of God's love

God has given us the spring to enjoy
As we should, like a child with a new toy
New life and promises are on their Way
As we follow the risen Jesus' day by day

As the open tomb does say
New life is budding forth that day
Cleansing us of wrongs we have done
By the glory of God's risen Son

**Thank You for the budding of new life and
Your risen Son this Spring day**

Buzz

First Snow

The first snow of the winter came last night
Surprising me this morning outside with a blanket of white
Covering the trees with a white coat too
Making the ground so white and new

When the sun arrive a white world was seen
Everything was covered so white and clean
The sun made the snow as brilliant as could be
Reflecting its light making it hard to see

The snow did not last very long that day
For the warmth of the sun melted the snow away
The snows on the trees are almost gone
Leaving the brown leaves withered and long

The sun turned the ground back to its earthy brown
As the melting snow disappeared from the ground
But patches of snow stayed in the shady spots
Escaping the sun's rays but not the warm air on top

The pure white snow and the brilliance of the sun
Reminded me of the purity of His Son
Nourishing the body and mind with His words
Of peace and love for all to be heard

As the snow melts and nourishes the ground
So too the Son nourishes our minds all around
Filling us with the love for mankind
As He guides us with words from His divine mind

Christ is like to snow so bright
Pure and glistening in the morning light
Melting our cold and sin away
Then guiding us through another day

**Thank You God for the first snow fall and
the nourishment from Your Son**

Buzz

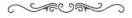

Food

Food, the substance of our life
It fills our daily needs
Giving us strength to continue
With stamina to go on our daily tasks

The breakfast cereal in the morning a beginning delight
A snack or lunch in the midday it fulfills the need
Relaxing dinner for the evening to sustain
The midnight repast to relax us to sleep

Yet the food of life I most desire
Is that, that comes from on high
That inner peace that fills the soul
Making me feel secure and whole

My meal comes in many forms
The eyes see the wonders of His creation
The magnificence of a mountain range high
A child at play

My ears hear the songs and sounds of the world
A flock of birds' communication on high
A cricket chirping in the moonlight
The bussel of a city street

The taste and aroma fill the mind
A sea breeze coming ashore
Crunch of a freshly picked apple
The sweet aroma of lilacs in bloom

The touch of a dog or cat passing through my legs
A chill fall breeze on the cheek
A splash of a cool mountain stream on the face
The feel of warmth of a blanket as I snuggle in bed

All and His Word are the food of life
For God did create them all
To enhance our life and replenish the soul
Bringing us closer to His Son, the Food of Life

Yes we need the physical food to keep us going
To strengthen us for the days ahead
For that is but a temporary fix
That holds the physical body together

For the food of life is a sustaining thing
Keeping us on a special Way
That can grow day by day
Keeping us healthy, a life on display

Thank You God for Your Creation and Your Son the Food of Life

Buzz

Footwear or Sandal of Sole

As footwear I am very close to the ground
For that is the place I am usually found
Covering the foot from the elements down here
Protecting them from damage with my gear

The family I come from has many branches
There are the loafers, tennis, dress, sandal and more
All come in many styles, colors, sizes and decor
Doing their jobs in all sorts of different ways

Cushioning the feet day after day
Smoothing the way they say
Some are quite stylish, others plain as can be
Feeling the ground that many do not see

Down here I see the world from an unique viewpoint
Either upwards or straight ahead
For the dust of the ground can cover my tops
And water can soak all my sides, what a shock

I am but a plain leather topped shoe
But I heard of a family member many years ago
He was called a Sandal of Sole, very fashionable in those days
Made of leather for there were no rubber soles they say

I would have liked to be that family member long ago
To protect the feet of the man he did know
This man was one of peace and light they say
Telling the people of a more humane Way

He did not travel very far from where He was born
He walked but thirty-three years but not alone
For many called Him Rabbi as they followed Him day by day
His last three years along those dusty back country roads

The story goes that Sandal of Sole even walked on water
As this man he shod went for a stroll
To visit His friends in a boat off shore
He said that he hardly got wet on that sea long ago

They say that Sandal tells of a wedding He did partake
That He changed water to wine that day
Of healing a man that came through the roof
Then telling others they needed no other proof

They say that Sandal of sole had many a story to tell
Seeing miracles from healing lepers to feeding a crowd
Talking to a lady drawing water from a well
Telling a story to children they listen, how swell

Sandal carried the man up a long road one day
To the top of a hill, a difficult way
They stripped off His robe and sandals too then crucified Him
For Sandal of Sole was lost in the shuffle that day

Sandal of Sole has been gone a long time ago
But his stories live on to this time we know
Of a man whose feet he did shield
And protected from the rough road He did trod

Sandal of sole was a servant of this man of peace
He carried and comforted His weary feet
Humble and loyal the ground he did trod
To carry that man with a message from Above

It many be the little things that we do
Providing something like comfort as humble shoes
It may be insignificant to you or me
For God can see compassion from you and me

Thank You God for letting us be servants to Thee

Buzz

Four Men

I meet four men the other day
Each very unique in every way
All had a tale to tell
They all told their story very well

These men of old wrote of events
They had experienced or had heard
Writing them down word after word
Of a man they knew so true

Telling of the man's life
How He cut to the truth like a knife
They started with His humble birth
Very unique to others on Earth

The story picks up when the man was about thirty
Of adventures and events by the sea
Miracles and Healing by the city wall
Dinner together with friends in houses and halls

Parables are told of events of life
How we should treat each other especially our wives
How to use our money and property too
And to love our neighbor as He does you

Stories of danger and intrigue are there
Betrayal and a parade to the temple square
As well as fulfillment of prophecies told
Of a man who was just thirty three years old

These four men are the Gospel writers four
Chapters and verses are an open door
To the teaching of a man that showed us the Way
How to live our lives day by day

To read these four books is an adventure you see
Into a new world of living for me
Four men of letters their stories tell
Of the Love of God they tell so well

**Thank You God for the Gospel Writers four
that tell of Your Love ever more**

Buzz

Friend

Many a verse has been written about a friend
A person true to the end
Someone whom you can console with
A person whom will get you out of a fix you're in

Acquaintances may come and go
As we travel to and fro
Meeting others as we go from place to place
Friendly encounters face to face

True friends many last for years
We always love to bend their ears
The distance may be short or far and wide
Yet in our minds they are by our sides

They help fill the days with peace and calm
For we know our friendship love lasts long
From crisis now and then
On them we can always depend

There is but one true friend I do have
He has stayed with me when I am sad or glad
Standing by me in thick and thin
Even through those ever changing whims

He guides me on my way
And helps me when I sometime stray
Giving me words of wisdom most every day
Leading me in His special way

I try to talk with Him everyday
As I place my life in His hands and on display
For I have never seen my faithful friend
My Lord and Savior, counselor, companion to the end

Thank You God for the friendship I have in Your Son

Buzz

Gloomy Day

I awoke this morning to a very gloomy day
The sun was not to be seen, it went away
Clouds covered the sky of blue, with a grey and off-white hue
The horizon had disappeared in a cloudy mist, too

Rain droplets hung all in a row on the eves outside
Waiting for the next droplet to push them down to the ground
Raindrops could be heard as they fall from the leaves above
Hitting and bouncing as they hit the roof overhead

Misty clouds covered the trees in the glen
Wrapping them so gently in a misty white shawl
Clouds above stretched as far as the eye could see
Hues of grey and white paint the covering clouds above

It is a gloomy, gloomy day I do see
Leaves on the trees are a dingy wet green
Branches are bending down drenched with rain
Grasses and flowers bow to the ground, a gloomy day

The day is shrouded in a white mysterious mist
Filling the air with the scent of new fallen rain
Obscuring the hills and valleys with low flying clouds
Hiding the sun from its daily trip overhead

But wait, is this not God's creation I see
The trees, flowers, grasses and animals are still here
The only difference is the clouds and rain
That nourishes the plants and animals to shine another day

For there are many phases of God's created world
Some sunny and bright some gloomy and cold
Yet all are creations of the Creator Himself
For us to enjoy be it gloomy or sunny

I enjoy this gloomy, not sunny day
For I may stay inside and read that time away
God has created all forms of days you see
For me to enjoy as any other created day will be

Thank you God for days that may seem gloomy for all are Yours

Buzz

God is here

God is here
Do not see Him anywhere
Where could He be
I know He is hiding behind a tree

I looked and He is not there
He must be a man for you say He is here
Ok just listen and hear with your ears
I hear nothing for He must not be near

Be quiet, close your eyes, what do you hear
Not much just sounds of Nature near
A bird out there is singing its song
A nice song, not very long

So what else do you hear
The sound of traffic and people nearby
Rustling of leaves as some animal passes by
A plane roaring by high in the sky

Now open your eyes and what do you see
Many many things around me
Flowers in bloom in a sea of green
A bright red rose that is stealing the scene

The pinwheel spinning in the sunlight
Flashing its colors so clear and bright
An insect just flew by
Gently moving across the sky

All those things you see, feel and hear
Tell me that God is near
For He is the One that created them all
From the biggest to the very small

So where is God you say
All around us, His creation is on display
A part of Him is in all that we see
Even all the parts of you and me

Thank You God for being near in Your creation so near

Buzz

Golden Morning

I woke up early the other day
The darkness of night had not gone away
Looking outside the darkness has started to pass
For I know that the morning would come at last

More and more the darkness faded away
Heralding a brand new day
Lighter and lighter the shadows they did fade
For soon the new day will be on display

Suddenly it did appear on the tops of trees
A golden light did I see
Coloring the crown on those mighty trees
A golden crown do I see

As the sun was rising
Through the forest leaves it did brighten
More and more the golden patterns spread
Illumining the forest in its golden glow

A patch of ground is of golden hue
Spreading its golden glow wider and wider
With more light the golden glow fades
As the morning sun rises in the eastern sky

Like the morning sun and its golden glow
The Son of Man brightens the souls of man on the earth below
Filling man with the wisdom of love and kindness
His light to the world has broken the darkness

Fulfilling the promise of God is love
That love for mankind will endure on the wings of the dove
For we are in the creation of God Almighty
Always present with us day after day

Thank you God for golden glow of Your Son

Buzz

Good Friday

Good Friday is finally here
We sit in silence before the program begins
Knowing its meaning and end
For the event has been told many times before

Silence brings the message to our memory
Steering the emotions of the event
Filling us with guilt and hope
For we know what will happen

Guilt, for we can do nothing, hope we can
For the past has gone and momentarily becomes the present
What could we have done
We are but bystanders living the events

We relive the trial, flogging and the long walk
Up the streets, we feel the guilt of our inaction
As the story unfolds we realize the end
What could we have done

Then we remember the real meaning of the day
A man has died for us and our sins
The way is now clear, to go forward again, another Way
Our understanding gives us new life through Him

Thank You God for jogging our memory on Good Friday

Buzz

Graduation

Graduation a time to move on
Leaving the past behind we go
Taking the next step in time
Leaving what we had done, to things to come

Graduation a time to move on
We celebrate the next step in education
The movement to a new school or career
A time to reflect on new and challenging tasks

Graduation a time to move on
A time we celebrate the youth
Going on to the next set of challenges
For parents whose jobs may almost be done

Graduation a time to move on
Yet we forget the ultimate graduation
The time others celebrate without us
For we have graduated to Heaven above

Graduation a time to move on
Life is an adventure with an inevitable end
A graduation we must attend, for it is
To be with our Father in Heaven an earthly end

Graduation a time to move on
A graduation to His Heavenly Home
To the Glory where we will go
And live in eternity in Heaven we will be

Graduation a time to move on
Memories will linger for those we must leave
We'll live on and on for them as they please
From photos or events will bring back the past

Graduation a time to move on
Slowly memories fade away
Replaced with new ones day by day
For others will never forget us, we are with our Father above

God Thank you for mortality, the Graduation and Your Love

Buzz

Green Caterpillar

A little green caterpillar did I see
Hanging from a tread swinging in the breeze
Climbing slowly as it was swinging in the air
I wonder if it had any earthly care

Up the thin thread it did climb
To where on leaves it would dine
Many of its friends are doing the same
For to them it is all a survival game

A game to survive the springtime
For if they survive this spring time divine
A cocoon will be their resting place
And days later merge as a butterfly, the cocoon it will escape

But where did this green caterpillar come from
An egg that was left last fall before the winter come
To lie in wait for winter to be done
And start to grow in the springtime sun

Then to emerge on a sea of green
To feast on the leaf to be far from lean
Then a cocoon for time to rest
Emerging as a butterfly its beauty the best

The butterfly flies from flower to flower
Pollinating flowers hour by hour
And when it work is done
Lays its eggs on a leaf, its job is won

We may think the event to nothing special
Yet in this little event life has occurred
For from His Very Word
Egg to caterpillar to butterfly a miracle did occur

The circle of life we have just seen
For God is there in the middle of the scene
Creating the system of Nature so fine
From His Power and Love Divine

Thank You God for Nature and the circle of life

Buzz

Hummingbird

The hummingbird, the hummingbird a small and mighty thing
Unique of all the birds on wing
Quick and agile of all birds I have seen
No other can hover by a flower so serene

They come in the morning to the feeder so red
In the cool of the morning they prepare for the day ahead
To dance from flower to flower in a dazzling display
Pollinating and feeding as they fly along their way

In the cool of the evening they come to the feeder red
To refresh and feed before the darkness begins
Then returning to the nest for a time to rest
To the trees above in their cozy nest

God did create this little hummingbird
Small in size and swift in flight
For in God's kingdom all are important
Your smallest deeds to others are important in God's eyes

Thank You God for the creature small that shows the way

Buzz

I Died

I died the other day
Memories of past days have passed away
Filling a book with things I did do and say
Telling of times and life as I went my way

Before I died I met a Man
Who said you can change your life, yes you can
Reliantly I listen to Him speak that day
Words of wisdom and encouragement without delay

He showed me my life in the past
Many things I had done to the very last
Then telling me of things that could have made me grow
And cleanse my past and restores my spirit and soul

For I died the other day
As He examined my soul and put it on display
Showing me a new and brighter new Way
For on that day I was reborn; He did say

The death of my past has gone to rest
For now my life has turned for the best
To follow a new and different path
A new life with hope and faith I will live to the last

I died that day, for Jesus Christ took me in
For He forgave me of my sins
Born again I follow His Way
Each and every day

Thank You God for my rebirth through Your Son

Buzz

Ice

Water in its hardest form clings to the river's banks
Shrinking and growing as the water flows beneath
White in its form against the darkness of the water below
Pieces floating; some swiftly, some gently on dark ribbons of water

Ice has crept across the river from rocky shore, to shore
Creating a bridge of white covering the water below
Stretching its whiteness along the slow moving river
Closing some of those black stretches of water flowing below

Some rocks impede the ice's flow
Sheets of ice pile up, one upon another, on rocks below
Creating ridges of ice toppie turbie in their display
Each one unique to the next one down the way

God has given us this ice we do see
To store up as liquid for His creatures and plants as they need
Stored in the winter for spring and summer you see
To melt and nourish the ground for the plants and creatures to grow

We thank God for the times of ice and snow
The times when the ground and air are cold
With the land covered in crystal white
Storing the liquid nourishment for later life

We Thank You God for ice of winter that stores water for spring

Buzz

Is Spring here?

The calendar says that Winter is still here
Although we are two months plus into the year
Snow in the mountains as white as can be
White the mountain tops against the blue of the sky I see

The snow which was once in the foothills on the ground
Has melted away leaving dead brown leaves all around
Bare branches still expose the trunks of trees
Yet small buds of life I percieve

As the days grow warmer and the sunlight lengthens
The once small buds begin to feel spring coming forth
Bursting forth from the buds: flowers emerge
As a myriad of new colors change the once dull winter scene

The flowers are as delicate as can be
Bursting forth for all to see
The glory of new life is now on display
Filling the waning of a Winter's day

The coming of Spring brings new life
A recreation to a once sleeping land
A new spirit of renewal of God's creation
For from death new life has begun

For new life has come with the Risen Son
His glory and work cannot be undone
For He guides us along His Way
To live in Paradise with Him one fine day

Thank You God for the coming of new life and Your Risen Son

Buzz

Is Winter here to stay?

The groundhog says the Winter is going to stay
Six weeks more, then Spring is on its' way
Blustery winds still fill the days
They say another winter storm is on its' way

The wind blows the dead leaves around
Twisting them on the oak; some may blown down
To the ground, so moist and wet
Covering the ground in a wet brown net

The light of daytime is longer now
Slowly increasing in the morning and evening hours
The sun warms the day with its rays of power
Awaking the ground for soon it will burst into flower

The warmth of the sun can be felt on me
Standing in the sunlight not in the shadows you see
Yet winter winds still cut the air
Ruffling my hat and even my hair

Small signs of Spring can be seen around
As the green stems of the crocus appear just above the ground
Pushing their leaves to sun and warmth above
For they are a sign of Spring stretching for the sun's warm love

Stirring within the branches are buds of new life
Waiting for the warmth of the sun is just right
To break forth into the Spring's new light
To shed its' protected cocoon and bursts out bright

God gave us this time to reflect
On the Winter we are in and that Spring is next
For the glories of His creation are all around
Be they the bleakness of Wintertime or the new life of Springtime

The days of Winter are numbered now
For some we will see the migrating fowl
Telling the lands that Springtime is on the way
And soon the groundhog will bask in the warmth of a Spring day

God has given us this season and more
His glory and creation we Praise and Adore
For the love of God has given us this time
To treasure and enjoy for this time is Thine

Thank You God for the Winter and the Spring to come

Buzz

A Lazy Summer Afternoon

A lazy summer afternoon I sit in the swing
Gliding back and forth viewing nature all around
Sunlight filters through the trees
As afternoon shadows slowly cross the ground

A light breeze caresses my face
As the breeze gently move the leaves of the trees
High in a neighboring tree leaves shimmer in the sunlight
Moving so gently in the afternoon light and breeze

The top of a pine sways gently back and forth
Like a metronome keeping time to the gentle breeze
The sounds of nature fill the air
As a crow or raven tells the world he is there

Silence is not a part of nature's way
The call of the birds as they make their way
A leaf falling gently to the ground
Hitting the ground with a cracking sound

The scurrying of a bird looking for a meal
A squirrel racing up a nearby tree
The fluttering of a windsock dancing in the breeze
Quail cooing as they gather to feed

A different scene as now when I first arrived
Shadows have moved, some longer others shorter
Sunlight on the ground filtered by the trees has changed shapes
Light now illuminates a spider's creation

Shimmering in the light the web glistens
A gentle breeze ever so slowly moves the threads about
And ever so slowly the strands vanish in the passing light
For will the web be there in tomorrow's light

God in His wisdom has created a wonderful scene
Filled with many wondrous things
Things we hardly see, hear or feel
We only need to stop and observe nature all around

**Thank You God for this time in the swing to
view a small part of Your Creation**

Buzz

Leaves of Fall

The leaves of Fall are rather wondrous
They feel the coming of the Autumn breeze
The shortening period of the waning sun light
And the coolness of the longer Autumn nights

The trees feel the same as Fall has come
It pulls back its nourishment to the leaves at its ends
Storing it in its branches, trunk and roots
Nourishment for the leaves in the Spring to come

The green of the leaves is slowly drained away
Slowly at first, as a few leaves change
More colors appear day after day
As shades of color coat the Autumn trees

Different trees display their wares in different shades
Some wear a single coat of color through the Fall
Others display two or three hues in all
While others wear a coat of many colors they do display

The display will last but a short time
For the breezes of late Fall and Winter will begin
To fill the air with their cooling gusts
Rustling the leaves to the ground below

Now the leaves of Fall will slowly glide
To the ground and in piles they do reside
Leaving the trees alone and bare
For soon the time of Winter will be here

Science can explain it all away
The color changes and the seasons too
All the processes that trees and leaves go through
From seed to tree and seed again

Yet where did it start so long ago
For God alone truly knows
He created the leaves and the universe too
The seasons and nature so definitely true

The splendor of the Fall leaves is a sight to behold
We see the changing of the seasons unfold
A wonder of the glory of God
Stop to enjoy the beauty of the God created for you

Thank You God for the season of Fall and its beauty so displayed

Buzz

Leaves

Looking outside the trees have bared themselves
The green leaves of spring and summer are gone
Some brown leaves of Fall cling to the seaming lifeless branches
Hanging and swinging in the winter's breeze

The ground is littered with many shapes of brown leaves
One upon another protecting the ground
Moving with the whims of the winds
Piling up against each other in waves of brown

Awaiting the coming of spring
New buds will come forth from the cold branches
Warmth from the sun will stir the host tree too
Fill its branches with the fluid of new growth

Small at first the buds will grow
Bursting forth in the warmth of springtime
Stretching out their buds now leaves of light green
Changing to darker green as the season matures

Now they have coated the once bare tree with leaves
Concealing most of their supporting branches
Bringing nourishment and life to its host with those around
Protecting those that make the tree their home

Leaves come in many shapes and sizes
Some star shaped some long and slim
Broad as a man's hand can be
Others grouped in a parallel design

Spring and Summer a wondrous time
Basking in the warmth of the sun
Being cleared by the rains that gently fall
And dried by the warm gentle summer breeze

Fall brings a change in the life of the tree and leaves
Slowly the nourishing fluids begin to dwindle
Colors of the leaves change with the on-coming season
The greens fade to yellows, reds and browns

The cool winds of Fall rustle the tree
Many a leaf floats to the ground below
With the cooler times more leaves will fall
Leaving but a few that cling stubbornly to their branch

Within this cycle life and death emerge
Following the cycle of nature's path
God has created this cycle we observe
Giving meaning to immortality we must acknowledge

For we also much follow this cycle
As the leaves on the trees follow their own
Giving life and nourishment to others
Doing the best we can with what we be

A Man called Jesus did the same you see
Followed the cycle of nature like you and me
But He gave us more in the time He was here
A new Way to follow that will always endure

Thank you God through the cycles of nature that show us the Way

Buzz

The Letter T

The letter T a letter it be
In words we have from A to Z
Giving the language we see and hear
In my case the language I read, speak, see and adhere

In this verse I write
The letter t is there in sight
Completing the words to meaning they be
Filling the sentence with T more than three

Then I look at the world around me
Many T's do I see
Telephone and power poles stretch from T to T
Bringing power and communication for you and me

The grid in a window there it be
Some streets end with a T
Afternoon passes a time we set for tea
Crossing contrails in the sky I see

Yet the T that means more to me
Is the T that was on Calvary
Who gives the Truth to you and me
That will guide us to eternity

For the T is a cross ✝ for me
Reminding us of that time on Calvary
Where a man I now know died for you and me
Forgiving our sins and setting us Free

Thank you God for T that is a Cross for you and me

Buzz

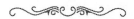

Light

The morning light streams through my window
Bringing forth its brightness to the room
Slowly warming the room with its flowing light
Moving the night shadows across the room

Looking outside to the world beyond the window
A new day is beginning as the light cuts the darkness of night
Spots of gold dot the ground as the light
streaks passed the trees and leaves
For some light has escaped the grasp of the trees

Mankind lives in the world of light
Avoiding the darkness and its fright
He takes the light into the night
Making the night cozy and bright

Man shines in the day with the light of the sun
Enjoying the light where work is done
Playing from dawn to dusk
Telling the hours by the position of the sun

Yet there is but one Light above all
Who shines brighter than any can recall
The Son of God is the Light for all
Lighting the world, and our lives, He will not Fall

For His Light has changed the world we know
Cleansing the mind and restoring the soul
Piercing the darkness of our unspeakable sins
Restoring the brightness, warming the soul, and making us whole

Thank You God for the Light of Your Son

Buzz

A Lighthouse

I saw a picture of a lighthouse the other day
A wonderful structure alone on display
Standing narrow and tall
With a wide base and this one with a white wall

It stands close to the rock shore
That passing ships so fondly adore
Spreading it nightlight far and wide
Guiding ships to safely pass by it rocky side

During those foggy nights and days
Its horn sounds its own melodic display
Saying here is a rocky shore so stay away
Guiding the ships from danger, be it night or day

Then I took a different look
And there it was in a familiar book
A lighthouse burning bright
Guiding human ships through their troubled nights

A humble yet divine man guiding us forth
Giving us the light to follow a new safer course
A course away from sin and decay
Guiding us to safer harbors on our way

Many a storm in life may pass
Yet the lighthouse gives safety that well last
Calming the waters during the storm
Bringing us to safe harbor in the arms of the Lord

Thank You Lord for the light that guides us in Your Way

Buzz

Like Snow Flakes

Slowly they drifted though the blue sky
Lazily falling as the breeze pushed them by
Floating gently on the breeze
Going here and there as they please

Looking skyward such beauty do I see
Splotches of white falling toward me
Like a crisp winter's day as the snow does fall
Bringing a new beauty to all

But it will soon be Summer and the days are warm
And Spring brings the occasional rain storm
So what are these white flakes I do see
Seed and pollen from a nearby tree

On closer view they vary in size
From marbles to peas with small seeds inside
Like a little delicate world they float by
Gently falling from the clear blue sky

A marvel of nature these fluff balls be
Spreading its seed to the ground we see
Finding a place to sprout and grow
One of many wonders from God you know

The wonders of God are all around
We need only to take time, so marvels can be found
Of God's creation of sky, earth and sea
Nature's gift for you and me

Thank You God for the little marvels of Nature we sometimes see

Buzz

Little Things

How often we forget about the little things
They are there every day
Present as we go on our way
At our beckon call be they big or be they small

I think of a shoe lace long and straight
Supply support for our shoes that lace
Keeping our shoes tight and secure
As we walk along we forget they are there

Pen, pencil, paper paperclip or pin
All important to life we live within
Keeping us organized and well on task
Making sure the things we do will last

For the little things we take for granite
Without them our lives would be chaotic
We use them and abuse them
Without them a lot more complicated our lives would be

Many more examples there be
All we have to do is look around and see
The glorious things that they all happen to be
Filling our lives with comfort we forget and need to see

And who gave us all these little things
Like the pencil and the string
The greatest Inventor and Creator of all
God who created the Universe so great and things so small

Thank you God for Your hands are in every thing

Buzz

Man In Stained Glass

The sunlight shines brightly as its rays pass through
Illuminating the stained glass's brilliant colors
Reds, blues, whites, and browns fill the scene
Bringing life and beauty to the view we see

There He is with out stretched hands
Greeting us all as we stand and see
The risen Christ in the stained glass view
For us Easter will always be a beautiful scene

His robe is as white as new fallen snow
Bathed in Heavenly Light from above a radiant glow
Arising on a cloud from the open tomb below
Conquering death with His power of Love

On closer view we can see much more
His right hand has a nail hole through and though
As well as the left hand and His feet also
Shattered stones at His feet show His power over death

For the risen Christ has conquered Satan's grasp
Bringing new life and a Way that will last
Forgiveness and Love are what He brings
Freeing us from our immortal sins

Thank you God for your Son and the sacrifice He made for us

Buzz

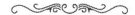

Medical Profession

The Medical Profession a noble profession indeed
We use their service when we bleed
To fix the hurts and conditions when the body is in need
Healing the body and mind they do to please

There are many a medical professionals we have
Treating ailments from a-z
With modern tools and some very old
Trying to make the body whole

They have a very complex job
For each body is a world of its own
Unique in size, gender or freckle on the nose
Complicating each ultimate diagnosis

They do the best they can
Asking for help from others at hand
Pooling their skills to heal the woman or man
Making the patient as healthy as they can

For God, The Master Healer, has given us those in medicine who care
They want to help and heal those in need
Healing and repairing the body of its disease
Bring health back to the body, a wonderful scene

**Thank You God for helping those who
can heal the body of its diseases**

Buzz

Memorial Day

Memorial Day a day we celebrate those whom have passed
It comes but once a year to honor
Those that served that are no longer here
They fought wars long past and present

We honor those who died to save us from tyrants
In days of past and even now
They gave their all to preserve a way of life so dear
Gone yet not forgotten for we remember them still

They fought for us to keep us free
Free from the rule of tyranny
To be safe in our land from the evils of man
Be it here at home or in a foreign land

They sacrificed their lives and body parts so we may enjoy
The freedoms we have and those we hold so dear
Near we not forget the price they paid
For we owe them a debt day after day

We thank You God for those who serve and have served
They keep us free in the land we love
Their sacrifices to keep us free
A sacrifice well known by Thee

Thank You God for this Memorial Day may we never forget

Buzz

Memorial Service

Attending a memorial service the other day
A celebration of life passed away
Who joined the Heavenly Father Above
In all His wondrous Love

Many came from far and wide
To express their sadness for the one that died
And of the joys they had with them
Of years past and as a dear and wonderful friend

We sang and heard songs they loved so well
Why they loved them they will not tell
Family members tell of adventures and fun
Of things they did and should not have done

Several would speak of times they had
Of times of sadness and times of glad
Accomplishments they had done before the day
Our friend passed away

The service is over and time does pass
Some memories will fade away; important ones will last;
Of the friend\companion who passed away
For in God's house we will see them some fine day

**Thank you God for those memories of those
who have joined your Heavenly Home**

Buzz

Moon Light

The moon shines forth its silvery light
Reflections from the sun so bright
Filling the night with its pale light
Illuminating as it slides on high through the night

With each coming night
Its changes its shape on its flights
Crossing the month from sliver to full
Then back to the time when it again is new

Giving the night traveler a light in the sky
A guide to the traveler which he/she can go by
Show the way through darkness display
Making unique shadows as a traveler is on his way

The disciples are like the moon you see
Reflecting the light of their teacher; Jesus He be
Showing us the light in the darkness around
With words and actions that are really quite sound

We look at the moon, a light in the night
Telling us of hope in the darkness not fright
For the light that shines from the Son on high
Guiding us forward out of darkness, like the night sky

**Thank You God for the moon and its reflected
light that reminds us of your Son**

Buzz

Morning Begins

The morning is a special time of day
It gets the day started on its way
Starting fresh from the night just passed
The morning has come at last

It begins near the darkest of night
With very faint slivers of light
Slowly, silently breaking the eastern sky
With faint but growing patterns they lie

Layers upon layers they increase in size
Slowly pushing the darkness across to the western sky
From the dark of night to gray then light blue
For the morning is coming all bright and new

Night shadows are gone as ambient light appears
For now we know the sun will soon be here
The quiet is slowly broken by the sun's rays
Crest the eastern horizon to start the day

The first golden rays touch the trees so high
Their tops golden against the blue sky
The golden rays are fleeting you see
For the morning has come with wonder they be

Scattered clouds announce the day as they reflect its rays
Hues of red, blue and light grays
Awakening the Earth for the new day is here
Another beautiful day has come this year

A new beginning so we can start this day
Created by God for us to grow and display
Our love of God and His Son our own way
Of His creation we see and hopefully say

Each morning a different display in a special array
Rays of light, clouds, and shadows
Each different in its own special way
Showing God's glory and creativity day after day

Thank You God for each morning so bright and new

Buzz

Morning Light

The morning light is about to return
For on the eastern horizon, a glow appears
Lighting the eastern sky with its wondrous glow
Painting the once darkness with pale light

The earth loosens its grip as the first rays appear
Cutting the late night shadows with its light
It paints the tops of trees and buildings with
The glow of golden light

As the golden rays find the ground below
Straight lines of light cut the lingering night's shadows
Making unique patterns on the ground below
Then filling the land with light so bold

For the morning has come and the quiet ceases
As the golden rays awaken the creatures of the day
Warming the land from its cool night's display
Awaking the land as it melting the morning dew away

For Jesus, our Lord, is like the morning Light
Taking away the shadows of doubt and despair
Warming the soul with care and peace
Lighting the Way to a brighter new day

**Thank You God for Your Son who brightens
the darkness of our lives**

Buzz

Morning Shadows

Morning shadows start before the morning light
They wait for the sun so bright
To rise in the east a wondrous new sight
The shadows cover the land as grayish delight

With the rising of the sun all will change
Rays of light cut the shadows into picture frames
Bright frames of light streak across the land
Bringing light to the once dark night

The morning shadows do not disappear
They move upon the land as the sun moves from here to there
Waxing and waning as the sun passes by
As shades on the land seeming to hide from the sun on high

As the morning shadows pass along their way
They change their name to the shadows of evening late in the day
As the setting sun casts its light
Longer shadows travel the opposite way a new delight

Now waning and waxing as the sun reaches the horizon
Then full shadows fill the land as the sunlight fades away
For dusk and night have returned a short time to stay
Shadows darken as night passes by

God did create this wondrous event
For us to enjoy, protect and accept
Nights, days, sunlight, and shadows
A world only You could create

Thank You God for Your creation around us, Thank You

Buzz

Morning Star

Going outside very early in the day
I saw the stars in the night sky on display
For the sun had not passed the horizon by
Flickering stars filling the Heaven high

There was one star that shone so bright
Among all the others in the dark night
They say it is the morning star
Shining its light possibly from very far

Then slowly comes pale light in the East
Slowly taking those stars away, rather neat
But the morning star shone ever so bright
The very last to leave the night

For the morning star is leading the way
Coming soon is a bright new day
A man long ago was like that morning star
Preparing the way for another man not very far

His name was John, a cousin of the other man
John preached repentance like no one can
He told of his cousin to come some day
Who would show us all a brand new Way

John preached to them by the river
Telling of a man to come who would deliver
Baptizing those who believed with Word and water
And telling of our Heavenly Father

For after the setting of the morning star
Comes the rising of the sun over the horizon not so far
Both the morning star and John tell of the brightness to come
Breaking the darkness with the power of the Son

Thank You God for the Morning Star

Buzz

Morning Sun

The morning sun has left its nightly rest
Leaving the covers of the horizon behind
Letting its ray fill the morning sky
As it climbs away for the horizon below

Over night the sky and clouds released the snow
Covering the ground and objects below
Coating the land with a blanket of white
Much to the delight of a cold Spring night

Now the sun is in command
Brings it warmth to the land once dark bland
Reflecting off the crystals so white
Creating droplets of water clear and bright

For the night creatures have return to their lair
As the day creatures come to the morning so fair
Enjoying the sun as it warms the day
Leaving tracks in the snow, what a display

Higher and higher the sun does rise
Stronger and stronger it light is no surprise
As it melts the snow that fell last night
Making this new day oh crystal white and bright

More and more droplets do appear
As the trees and bushes shed their coats of white
The coat that they got in the early morning night
Slowly bearing their branches to the sun's light so bright

God's world is a wonderful thing
Be it Fall, Winter, Summer or Spring
All we need to do is open our eyes
And see the glory of God's creation, no lie

Thank You God for the morning light and beauty of your creation

Buzz

Mother and Child in Stained Glass

A Stained glass window an unique picture to see
Not a black and white or colored photo it be
Or a canvas of watercolors or oil you see
But of lead and pieces of colored glass together it be

Each window is unique in its own way
Changing from day to day
As light passes through its colored pane
Reflecting light in a very unique way

The window I see is simple to view
A scene of a mother and child, brand new
She holds the child with tender care
Counting her blessing for her to share

A window of stained glass I do see
Mary and Baby Jesus they be
Sheltered from the cold of night
In a stable wonderfully bright

A cow and donkey watch from not so far
The cow wondering who these strangers may be
Who have invaded her home this cold night
Using her feeding trough as a bed for this baby

The donkey explains to the cow this night
Of a long journey that brought them this way
To the City of David to be counted that day
And his pregnant lady he did carry a long way

A bundle on the floor tells a story also
Of a long trip to this place and city you know
For the journey did not end at a comfortable inn
But in this stable where a cow resides inside

A star shines brightly above this scene
Lighting the night with its heavenly glow
Companioned by many to light the night
Warming the night with its Holy Light

To the left of the bright star above the stable small
Faint images of angels here may be
Watching over this glorious scene
For a special gift was given that night

For this is the child that the prophets foretold
That would be born in the city of David of old
To save us all and show us the Way
To a Brighter and Glorious new day

God gave His Son to live with us on Earth
To show us the Way to follow from that day forth
That love and forgiveness are the Way we should follow
For The Comforter will always be with us from our birth

Thank you God for that first Christmas night and gift

Buzz

My Human Body

My human body, the place I stay
Been with me for many a day
It is with me in the day light
And stay with me through the night

In my youth it was an active thing
Going places and doing things, even at times on a swing
Bumps, burses, cuts and scrapes my body did encounter
Shoveling snow from the walk, outside for many an hour

School kept me busy through the college days
Then sending me on into the world and its new ways
Jobs were there, they taught me much
Telling me times to slow down, other times to rush

My body it did endure, the demands I did make
Helping me grow older yet I still made mistakes
Colds and flu, cut and scrapes all along the way
Allowing me to get stronger, wiser and old, day by day

But there was one thing that keeps me in tow
Besides a wife and children, you know
The voice in the back of my mind
Said to do the best you can all the time

For I am a child of the 50's and 60's they say
Told by adults to listen and obey
Do the best you can, night and day
Follow the Golden Rule, and do what it does say

God gave me life many years ago
I try to follow the rules to keep me in tow
To live by a creed that honors God and man
And be a good steward of God's created sea and land

He gave me a book to follow if I can
And live by His Son's parables and still have fun in the sand
The parables gave me words of wisdom for they are words to live by
All down to Earth, not pie in the sky

For my body and mind are a gift you see
From God to me to be the best I can be
To care for it as best I can
For my life, is always in God's hands

**Thank You God for the gifts, You have
given me and the body I possess**

Buzz

New Years Day

Another year has gone away
A new year begins on New Years Day
The old year has become history passed
And into history be written at last

Many memories of the last year we see
Happiness, sorrow, joy and despair, they all be
Traveling through the mind those memories unique
Reminding us of the happening in the year now complete

We tend to forget the blessing we did receive
The little ones that came to you and me
We got out of bed most every day
The sunlight that warmed us as we went our way

Food and meals we all enjoyed
Conversation with friends we did employ
Sounds of songbirds on the wing
The aroma of spring flowers; the breeze did bring

Many a blessing has passed our way
They came to us each and every day
So as a new year has just begun
New memories we need to collect one by one

God gave us another year
To venture into, without any fear
For He is always with us by our side
As with His Son we shall abide

**We Thank You God for this New Year
and the adventures it will bring**

Buzz

Night Sounds

I opened the window the other night
Before the moon had spread it light
A cool breeze caressed my face
Almost like a piece of fine silk lace

Then it came to me as I looked outside
The darkness had taken the world away
The sounds and view of the day were gone
And a new world outside has now dawned

The eyes could not make out much at all
For the night had cover the day like a high wall
The difference was very profound you see
For night cover was there, and there it be

New sound filled my ears that night
Even without the light
Crickets could be heard in the darkness
Their sounds told me they were out there in the blackness

Then another sound found my ears
I could not identify, be it frog or deer
Adding to the sounds of the crickets near
It made a rib it sound, a frog, nothing to fear

The night sounds have a melody all its own
Something that you would like to clone
Peaceful, calming low and sweet
A rhythm that is about to put me to sleep

For God make these night sounds
To fill the night all around
To calm the body, preparing it for sleep
Relaxing the mind for sleep to be deep

Thank You for the cooling, calming night sound before we sleep

Buzz

November Day

The daylight is shorter now
As fall comes into full swing
The trees and leaves are doing their thing
Preparing for the time to rest before spring

Leaves begin to change their color of green
To the many shades in the autumn scene
Yellow, gold, red, black, and shades of brown
Coats of many colors, fall trees all around

The sun is lower on the horizon these days
Entering the day later each morning
Leaving sooner with its afternoon light
Warming the day slowly as it crosses the fall sky

The animals prepare for the winter to come
Some leave for warmer climates, some before the day is done
Others prepare their nest with food to maintain
Heavier coats are the fashion for others, the winter to sustain

For this month is a time to remember
For now the harvest is done
Stores of plenty we have received
For the time of Thanksgiving is near, hard to believe

A time to count the blessing of the year
No matter they be good or ones we did fear
All blessing from God we shall be glad
For blessing come with eternal love from our Heavenly Dad

God gave us many blessings
So many we can hardly list or comprehend
We need only look around and see
Blessings upon blessings He has given, greater than the sea

**Thank You God for November to remember
Your countless blessings**

Buzz

November, A time to Celebrate

November has come and is almost passed
Thanksgiving Day, new memories will last
Of family and friends near and far
Sharing a table of Blessings above par

The table was set so we all gathered around
Each to his/her place we all found
Each setting a beautiful display
In Fall colors like colors of the day

With the aromas of Thanksgiving filling the room
Of turkey, dressing, green beans and pumpkin pie coming soon
Our table is blessed with bounty for the day
With family and friends and memories that will stay

We celebrate the harvest we planted in Spring
Our tender care brought it full swing
To a harvest of plants on the land that God did provides
With the help of God right by our side

He gave us the land, the seed and the rain
Working the land with skill and pain
Toiling from day to day
Working toward the harvest we now have on display

We may not be a farmer who tills the land
But we all work with His plan
To provide for our family with God's helping hand
Be it housewife, accountant, carpenter or handy man

God has provided us with many talents you see
To be the person that He wants us to be
For Thanksgiving is a time we need to reflect
On the many Blessing the past year we do possess

God thank You for Thanksgiving and the blessing You have bestowed

Buzz

November Winter Approaches

November has come and is almost passed
For the thirtieth is the day last
It came in as a light Fall breeze
Ending with a cold wind that shakes the trees

The leaves started the month mostly green
Now all are mostly golden brown, a beautiful scene
Some have turned red, with shades of green. tan and yellow
Carpeting the ground, a spectacular colorful scene so mellow

The ground was once light brown before the rain
Now it is like milk chocolate brown, very hard to explain
The trees were once covered with leaves
Now bare with brown branches is all I see

The wind came up the other day
Blowing leaves and snow all different ways
Telling the creatures to take shelter until the storm does pass
For winter is approaching, with a more fearsome blast

But why do we have this November surprise
To prepare us for an event that will brighten our eyes
An event so spectacular it cannot be contained
The birth of a child on Bethlehem plain

It may have happened many years ago
Yet the story and event never gets old
An event that changed the world we know
To a new Way, a new world, so on we will go

Thank You God for preparing us for a season of change

Buzz

October

October is a month in flux
Filled with surprises, very much
From a day of cold to one hot like a Summer day
A month of transition, in a very colorful display

This month is in the midst of change
With longer nighttimes and shorter lighted days
For Fall has arrived in this colorful display
Chilling the night yet warmer during the day

With changes day after day
October has many things to say
Telling the creatures to prepare to leave or stay
For Winter is coming not far away

Those who stay will prepare for the Winter blast
Storing their supplies, planning for them to last
Preparing their nests or dens to sustain
Their food and shelter from the Winter's stinging pain

Some will leave and head to warmer places
Going far from the Winter's blast
Walking or flying to a place secure and warm
Staying awhile until the Spring tells them "no more"

Some birds will fly south in formation, very neat
For those who stay their Winter coats near complete
The leaves fall to protect the ground
As the days takes on a different sound

The sound of birds as they declare their way
The cricket chorus softer than yesterday
Crunch of the fallen leaves under foot
The thump of an acorn as it hits the roof

For the harvest is complete
The stores are all safe and secure
For now it is time to count the Blessings
Of the bounty that has just occurred

We owe it all to the Almighty One
Who gave us the land and knowledge to plant
The tools and practices to use the land
To grow the bounty and harvest the crops

For October is God's gift to us
A time to prepare for the Winter to come
A gift of a plentiful harvest we need to share
As well as a time to remember from whence it comes

Thank You God for October and the bounty of the harvest

Buzz

Passover Room

There was a festive feeling in the air
For hundreds of people had come into the city
Another religious holiday was about to begin
Filling the city as it had done time and time before

Earlier that day the room had been prepared
Cushions were in their proper places with low tables too
Plates and goblets were neat and trim
For tonight the feast would begin

There were an odd number of settings that day
Thirteen were counted, hope they all stay
Sunset was approaching fast
As lengthening shadows crossed the room and passed

Then I heard them coming up the stairs
Discussing the events of the day
Entering the room and taking their places
Ready for that evening Passover meal

The man at the head of the group
Said a blessing before the meal was brought forth
He followed the tradition set forth long ago
But He washed their feet to the objection of one

They all dined on the meal before them
With more conversation of the day's events
Unleavened bread, lamb, hors doeuvers and wine
A traditional Passover feast done the traditional way

A silence came over the room after the meal was done
The leader began to speak and all were intent
Listening to His words that He spoke that night
Filling the others with sorrow and puzzlement

This man took some bread, broke it and
Said this was His body, a curious thing to say
Then taking a cup of wine He spoke this way
That the wine was His blood shed for them always

He said to do this to remember Him
A curious statement for what did He mean
Was he going away, He did not say
Then one of the men left and the rest did stay

Later that evening all got up and left
Following their leader down the stairs
Leaving the room to the darkness they went
Did they leave without paying the rent

Through the windows the next day
Came an unusual set of sounds
The jeering of the crowds
As men passed below on the road

When they had passed the normal sounds returned
The day continued as days had before
Then darkness filled the room
An eerie feeling never felt before

Later was heard that the leader from the night before
Was crucified that day on a hill far away
They say He carried the world's sins that day
That saved the people who would follow His Way

As followers who follows His Way
We remember that room and the meal that day
Celebrate that meal as Communion today
We do this in remembrance of Him

Thank You God of a Passover feast long ago that changed us all

Buzz

Passover

A religious holiday of remembrance we celebrate
A holiday that has no specific date
For from year to year it changes its place
For in March and April is its wandering home

Passover celebrates an event many years ago
When the Hebrew were told to go
To leave a land they knew for years
And travel to a new land of once they heard

A man called Moses was called by God
To set his people free
From the Pharaoh of Egypt long ago
The Hebrews were slaves you know

The Pharaoh would not let them go
So God sent seven plagues all in a row
To soften the will of the King
For each plague was a horrible thing

The last plague was a deadly one
That took the first born sons
But the Hebrews were protected by the blood of a lamb
Placed on the door frame by hand

The meal that they had that faithful night
Was one of the last before their flight
They remember that meal to this very day
In a very traditional way

Bitter herbs and unleavened bread
The meal they had before bed
For they needed to be ready to go
For this time the Pharaoh did not say No

The tradition has been passed on
From ages and ages, father to son
From times of plenty
To time of none

For Passover is a time to remember
Of the events that occurred many years ago
The tradition we must keep in toe
And the sacrifices our forbearers did know

God gave us Passover to hold and keep
To remember cherish and even weep
For the sacrifices, that they endured
That brought us the Word

Thank You God for the tradition You gave us, Passover

Buzz

Rain

After a long period of dry
The rain came before the plants could die
It came in first as a moist aroma in the air
Then ever so gradually clouds and a mist did appear

As the clouds darken above
More misty droplets began to tickle my face
They changed the ground from light to darker brown
Covering the leaves with a clear wet sheen

Puddles in low places slowly fill, as the rain increases
Cleaning the air as it sweeps the dust away
Little streams appear as the rain trickles down the hill
Joining others as they slowly fill the streams

In the house I could hear it hit the roof
Like fingers drumming on the table top
More and more the rain did come
Sliding down the roof to fall over the eves

Falling once again to the ground below
Some slid off the roof through the gutters they went
Taking the long way to the ground below
Down through a tunnel then out on the ground

Leaves, trees, buildings and such
Impede the raindrops to their ultimate end
Taking their part of the nourishing and cleansing rain
Yet letting go most to the ground below

Rain is a blessing from above
As it cleans the air and nourishes the land it touches
Nature is God's way to bring life
Quenching the thirst of a parched land

Thank You God for nature and the rain it does provide

Buzz

Robe

A robe is an outer garment to protect the wearer
Over the years it has taken several forms
Covered many a person now and then
Some royal but mostly humble men

Long and flowing some almost touch the ground
Some with hoods to cover the head
Some may possibly conceal a smile or a frown
In a rainbow colors they can be found

Royalty wear them well
Common folk wear them for warmth you know
Protecting them from winter's blast
Or the pelting rain as spring storm does pass

Long ago the robe was accentual
A garment of the day
Protection from the storm
And warmth for the coolness of a night's stay

A young man wore a seamless robe
As He walked the streets and roads of old
To tell people of a new Way to live
Filled with hope and words that forgive

He told of laws of the day
How they were manipulated by the Pharisees and Sadducees
They would say this is the way to the Almighty God
Give us money so you would be saved

This peaceful man told of another Way
He came to fulfill the laws of old
And to love one another as He loves us
To Honor God in all that you do and say

The establishment did not like His message
It broke up the traditions they had put forth
They said that this man had to go
For what He said was Truth and Life to the soul

They figured a way to get rid of this man
And so they did with a despicable plan
A mock trial was the scene
Guilty by blasphemy they said that day so mean

The warmth of the robe was stripped away
Beaten and taunted that very same day
Then displayed with a robe of regal display
Then devised ways to crucify Him on a hill far away

His original robe was put over His wounds again
As He carried His cross to that hill far away
To be stripped of His robe once again
For He was crucified that day

His robe was discarded on a pile of stuff
For lots were cast for that robe He just wore
One soldier got that robe for not much
For they thought He would die and need it no more

We do not know what happened to the robe that day
For they took the man down to a tomb where He was lain
That day did pass and another one too
His tomb was empty the morning next

For the Lord God Almighty had raised Him that day
Giving new life to the world to stay
For we follow that man to this very day
Following Him in a new Way

We may or may not have a robe that we own
To keep us comfortable and warm
Yet we never forget that time long ago
Jesus died for our sins and His Spirit is with us this very day

Thank You God for the clothes to wear provided by you

Buzz

Rock Wall

Saw a rock wall the other day
Extending along the ground a long way
Not that high but high enough
Keeping things in and out, a job quite tough

Some rock walls are as thick as can be
Others low and hard to find and see
Most are pleasant and grand they be
Still others harsh and cruel to you and me

Some rock walls are made of colors bright
Others with holes to let through the light
Some with uniform rocks of the same size
The one I saw had all different rocks supplied

Rock upon rock they all form a wall
All sizes and shapes from boulder to pebble small
Some walls not very straight or level
All changing our paths as we go along our way

There are many rock walls in my life
Removing them would be a great delight
Worry, fear, and others walls that needs to go away
Then I can start a new glorious day

You can take down that wall
All you need to do is to ask and call
For He will help you breach that wall
One rock at a time with His help the wall will fall

Jesus will help but you must believe and try
And the rocks will fly
Despair, sin, worry and the like
As you and He remove the wall, pushing it out of sight

Thank You God for your Son and His Way to remove my walls

Buzz

Rocks

Rocks, rocks, rocks all I see
On both sides of the train by me
Many sizes and shapes these rocks maybe
Some hanging on slopes very precariously I see

Some in layers and layers upon layers
The layers maybe straight as can be
Others layers point to the sky
Looking at them I wonder why

Other rocks are oval or round as can be
They say they are river rock heading to the sea
Bounced along the river's bed
Not a very good place to lay my head

Besides the river the wind moves the rocks along
Cracking their faces and wetting them down
Eventually to fall to the ground, far below
Sometimes alone or with a group they go

Rocks together build many things
Walks, roads, towers, dams, and to hold in a spring
Castle walls thick as can be
Or a fence, some as long as you can see

Yet there is a rock that stands all alone
A man who was told to build a new home
For a new Way of thought, a brand new Way
To serve the Lord the right way, each and every day

We also must try to be like Peter, the rock
True to the Lord around the clock
Building our faith as rock solid as he
Spreading Jesus' message from sea to shining sea

Thank You God for the rock, its beauty and our foundation

Buzz

Sanctuary

A sanctuary is a place to be
Where life is safe and free
From the dangers that pass which we feel and see
Secure in a place where comfort and security be

Over the years there were many sanctuaries I have seen
As a child in the care of my parents; that was home for me
At school the rooms where I learned and grew
That gave me knowledge to waylay my fears or woes

Then in young adulthood the position I had
A place where I belonged with a job I did well
For sanctuary was the peace of mind I possessed
Of the people who helped me in the position I had

Many things have been a sanctuary for me
Home, family, work and church, they be
Filling a void when I was lost or alone
Removing the clouds of darkness and gray away

Over the years some sanctuaries have changed
Once bright and happy; now gloomy and dark
A new sanctuary has replaced those which have fallen
That brightened my day with peace within my all

Yet there is one sanctuary that is more important to me
That is the sanctuary with God, The All Mighty
He gives me peace and comfort each and every day
His Son to guide me along the Way

His sanctuary is always close at hand
Always there when I need A Friend
Carrying me through to a peaceful end
Cradling and loving me all of my days

Thank You God for being my Everlasting Sanctuary

Buzz

School

We all go to school from the day we are born
Some of us would like to scorn
Yet we have a tendency to learn every day
Some things we tend to keep, other we throw away

Into our minds the learning flows
A little at a time, so more we know
As a child very young, what things can I do
And other things are against the rule

As we grow older the knowledge will increase
The three R's, the Golden rule studies unique
Sometime slowly, other times quickly into the ear
Filling the mind with facts, some cloudy; others clear

Through the travels of life
Schooling is never out of sight
Be it the school of hard knocks
Or the ways to get in and out of a verbal fight

For every day we may learn something new
Or from our mind glean something to use
The learning is always for us to see
On land, in the sky, or at sea

The school of experience we sometime enjoy
Learning from events to and fro
Trying not to make mistake from the past
Hoping that our decision will last

For the school of life is here to stay
With us each and every day
School can be fun if we take time
To enjoy learning as a lifelong design

And who gave us the concept of school
Our Creator, Head School Master, teacher too
He gave us a mind to explore and see
The creation around us is available for you and me

He gave us the our mind and school you see
To be independent and a community be
To learn from each other on our way
Attending His glorious school day by day

Thank You God for our time in eternal school

Buzz

Seasons

There are four seasons that visit yearly
Changing the landscape as they pass by
Coloring the lands in their specific hues
And each one different in its unique way

Spring brings us the time of new birth
Buds, flowers, creatures and trees
Burst forth in a new display
They brighten the land as a fresh new day

The bare branches of a deciduous tree
Bud and a light green leaf comes forth
The young venture out on spindly legs
As the young chick takes to wing

Summer brings us the time to mature
Fully-grown are the plants and creatures now
Enjoying the warmth of the daily sun
Relishing the coolness of an evening breeze

The longer daylight helps ripen the grain
Those once fruit blossoms let fruit slowly appear
The warm water lakes give relief from the heat
And people enjoy a relaxing day at the beach

Fall brings us the time to prepare
The harvest is near and creatures are aware
The stores are secure with a chill in the air
As those that must leave head on their way

A chill in the air quickens the pace
The harvest is near and school is in place
Watching the leaves as they color and fall
And skyward they fly as V's on the wing

Winter brings us the time to conserve
We slow down as the cold of winter is here
To eat of the harvest and think of spring
And celebrate the birth of a King

Flakes upon flakes fall from the sky
Growing icicles hang from the eves
Hot chocolate and marshmallows are there to please
And the holiday season has just passed us by

Two seasons seem longer than most
The winter with its daylight so short and cold
And summer with its daylight so long and warm
Both seem to last for a very long time

While fall and spring seem to not linger at all
Buds come quickly and burst into bloom
Trees in the fall change colors to soon
And quickly they scatter their leaves on the ground

The seasons are like life within me
Birth, to youth, mature and rest
Passing from one to the other a wonderful quest
As we see the seasons pass for the best

But who gave us this glorious array
Seasons that change and brighten the days
That explains the cycle of life in a beautiful way
The Creator of All, yes God Almighty do I say

God you have given us the seasons, their beauty so magnificent

Buzz

Shepherd in Stained Glass

They say a picture is worth a thousand words
So then a stained glass window would surely be heard
Colors a many enhanced by the light
Telling a story to be viewed vary so bright

I viewed a window the other day
Simple in design yet lots to say
Framed with glass of red and green
Ever changing as the light and hours passed this scene

The window showing me a pastoral scene
A Shepherd stands tall with His staff in hand
At His feet sheep in a little band
With a new born lamb cradled in His arm so serene

In a pasture green by a sky blue stream
Gently flowing through this peaceful scene
Mountains and hills behind them all
Below a canopy of a clear blue sky

On closer view the sheep were of different shades
Some tan, white and reddish-gray were their fleece
The Shepherd dressed in white as white as can be
Tending His sheep with compassion and care I do see

The stained glass window is of Jesus as a Shepherd
Tending His flock in a setting of pastoral assurance
Shepherding His flock of many shades
Giving them directions as the Way they may follow

Not one who knows the Shepherd will be left behind
Caring for the very young and the old in time
Guiding them through the rocky places
Providing them with pastures green

The Shepherd is here to guide us all
No matter what color or hue we many befall
Or how old or young we may be
Guiding us with care as you can see

We may lose our way from time to time
But He is there to help us find
The path that He did design
Always in His loving arms sheltered there we be

Thank you God for Jesus our Shepherd that shows us the Way

Buzz

Sierra Nevada in Winter

The Sierra Nevada Mountains, a wonderful sight to see
Of rocks, trees and snow there be
Around every curve a new view for me
Different rock formations, snow and trees

They can be seen from afar
From the high desert in the east
To the inland valleys in the west
Reaching high into the sky

For miles upon miles they set the western valleys aside
Going north and south the land they divide
A mighty range some ten thousand feet high
With many a lake and valley hidden inside

For winter has come, it is that time of year
The snow has covered the ground
From trees to rocks all around
With a blanket of white some places higher than a deer

The tops of their peaks are as white as can be
Stretching as far as the eye can see
Punching holes in the blue sky above
With snow on top the skiers so dearly love

The higher we go the deeper the snow
Giving the land a definite white glow
Snow on the branches bends them down low
Some lower branches reaching the ground below

Tracks in the snow says, something was there
May be a fox, bobcat, deer or a hare
Looking for food somewhere out there
Finding some so the stomach is not bare

The Great Loving Creator did all I do see
Ever changing the scene for thee and me
How great is His creation be
The Sierra Nevada a wonderland I do see

Donner Lake Sierra Nevada

Thank You God for the wonders of Sierra Nevada in the Winter

Buzz

Signs

We live a world of many signs
They come in many sizes and designs
Tell us what to do and where to go
What is coming and what we may know

They tell us of the past
Even where to pass
How high we happen to be
Even how close we are to the sea

Signs tell all sorts of things
When we get to fly and take to wing
How high or low to sing
And when to go to the Dr. because of a hurting sting

A sign maybe seen by the eye
Or maybe a feeling that does, not go by
A sound in the air of danger near
Or of an aroma of something to fear

Yet there are signs in a book I have read
That tells of stories that stir the head
Of people of long ago just like you and me
That saw the signs and followed, the LORD Jesus, even across the sea

His signs were told in parables, the Bible does say
Of ways we should live each day
To take care and respect God's creation at hand
Even respect our fellow man

The sign I like from God the most, you see
Is that He loves me as I be
Imperfect in several ways
For I try to follow His Way, day by day

Thank You God for the signs, You provide to guide my way

Buzz

Silence

Silence is a beautiful thing
A word not spoken
Thoughts not orally exchanged
A voice not heard

In silence the senses come alive
Ears hear sounds not before heard
They come forth much more clearly
Telling us the world is really near

The sound of a deer rustling the leaves
Mating call of a frog in shallow pond
Leaves rustling in the afternoon breeze
Birds wakening with the morning sun

The eyes can see clearer than before
Details that were unseen now appear
Sharper and clearer than ever before
Filling the senses ten times more

A rose with petals shedding the morning dew
Clouds sliding by on a moonlit night
Shades of colors on an autumn day
Snow on a mountain peak far away

The nose comes alive as it savors the air
Filling its passages with a freshness after a spring rain
A pungent aroma of fresh baked rolls
The aroma of lilac in full bloom

Silence for mankind is an interesting thing
It can be tough love or deep love
Respect or avoidance silence can be
And golden moment between you and me

For silence is where the senses are
Filling them with the world near by
Awaking the mind to where we are
In a creation not that far

In the silence there is a sound
The sound of God all around
Filling the senses we have forgotten
A beauty that only can be found in God's creation

**Thank you God for the beauty of silence
we can see, hear, smell and feel**

Buzz

Snow

The white form of the water it be
Flakes as thin as paper you can see
They say not two flakes are the same a challenge to me
Each a crystal as delicate as can be

They float to the earth from clouds fluffy white
Gently floating from the heavens above
To land safely on the cold ground below
Flake upon flake they blanket the ground

One upon another till the brown ground is gone
Hundreds of thousands of flakes they do fall
Becoming a crystal white blanket several inches tall
Everything around has a white coat of snow

Steep hills are an interesting sight to behold
As snow slides or rolls to the base down below
Tracks in the snow tell of traffic afoot
Creating unique patterns as they break the blanket's smooth flow

We come upon a river a wide path it be
She is covered with ice and snow as flat as can be
Rushing water below creates an opening as black as ink
Creating ice forms so many both thick and thin

The winds play with the snow in interesting ways
At times the winds blow fast and free
Making the world outside hard to see
And other times falling gently to pile the snow in drifts that flow

The sun on the snow is such a delight
As we travel along it reflects a sparking light
Like the twinkling of stars on a cloudless night
Creating the snow to be a brilliant white

Snow is winter's blessing from God above
Cooling and protecting the ground on which it lies
Storing moisture for times to come
Casting its beauty to the land below from Our God Above

Thank you Lord for snow that protects and nourishes, as do Thee

Buzz

Spring, a New Time

I stepped outside the other day
Viewed a new beautiful world on display
An awakening world invaded by senses
Of the new world now in bloom

The aroma of the purple lilac filled the air
A sweet perfume I do declare
That sweetens the mind of an aroma scent
Cleansing the air with its lilac scent

Colors filled my eyes that very day
Greens and reds, yellows and blues
Replacing the browns of the winter's gloom
Brightening the day as Spring colors do

Upon my ears are new sounds
Different sounds of birds all around
The crickets chirp their melodious theme
While frogs can be heard croaking in between

The scenes come alive in Spring you see
More birds have arrived on this day
More colorful than those of the winter blend
Colors as beautiful as the rainbows bend

God did create this yearly scene
To remind us of a living past event
Of the coming of a new Way
That is with us this very day

A new Way to view the world around
A Loving God is with us this very day
Forgiving indiscretions we do display
Guiding us on a more forgiving Way

Thank You God for the renewal of your Way

Buzz

Spring Breeze

A spring breeze passed my way
Making this day a delightful day
Weaving it way through the trees and grass
Slightly cooling the land as it did pass

Its cousin and others did pass months ago
For cold and biting the winter breeze did blow
Then I knew it would not last
Soon spring breezes will come and winter passes

Spring breezes are a delight to behold
Gentle and sweet not too hot or cold
Bringing the aroma of fresh grown flowers
As their sweetness fills the evening hours

Its warmth brings the plants to bloom
Out of their winter cold and gloom
Warming the air and ground as it passes gently by
Gently pushing the clouds on high

The spring breeze also brings the spring rain
Falling so gently on the mountains and the plain
Giving nourishment for the new grasses to grow
Cleaning the leaves with a wet new glow

The invisible breeze we see its display
As it passes through leaves on its way
To warm the land here and far away
Telling us that spring and new life is here to stay

As I sit here and enjoy the spring breeze
A thought occurs from my head to my knees
That God created all that I see and hear
Be it far away or so very near

God created the spring breeze
He, likes the breeze it is a comfort to me
Giving me strength to last through the day
Guiding me along His Way

The warm of His Love helps me to grow
As I try to follow His path with my sinful soul
For the spring breeze is but the breath of God
Warming the soul with His forgiveness, mercy and Love

Thank You God for the spring breezes and Your Love

Buzz

Spring, Here at Last

The season of Spring has finally come
For the Winter calendar is defiantly done
The daily sun and its light are staying longer
With its sunny rays getting stronger

Signs of Spring are beginning to show
With blossoms on some bushes and trees beginning to grow
In the valley below the trees are budding light green
Changing the land to a beautiful colorful scène

The chilly winds of Winter come less often these days
In the cloudy and rainy storms that pass quickly on their way
For the warmth of Spring is slowly getting the upper hand
Warming the days and warming the land

The still wet ground that once was covered with snow
Has new life that will grow from the earth below
For breaking the ground are shoots of plants green
That are delicate and coming onto the Spring scene

As the calendar days of Spring continue to come
Creeping up the foothills more and more Spring has begun
Yet high above the valley and foothill Winter is not done
For mountains of white can be seen sparking in the sun

Buds of new life come onto the scene
Filling the bushes and trees, tiny buds are seen
Soon to burst forth in the warmth of the sun
Bringing color, life and Spring time fun

God has given us Spring to refresh our lives
To see the world new with clearer eyes
The renewal of life from a once dormant land
As we see new life at our stretched out hands

Spring envisions the coming of a new start
The time of dormancy has passed
New life is beginning to emerge from the cold dark ground
Warmth is replacing the bitterness of Winter

For life came from a cold dark tomb
Which burst forth from the depths of dumb
Bringing new life and light to the plight of man
For through Jesus and His Way, we can

For the Light of Love shown brightly on Easter day
Filling the land, for Love was on display
Bringing new life and meaning to mankind
For now we know and feel that Love is from the Divine

Thank You God for the Springtime and the creation of new life

Buzz

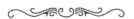

Spring Not Far Away

Spring may not be far away
Per the calendar just a few more days
Even though there is snow on the ground
Patches of brown ground can be seen all around

For in the morning light a group of flowers were in sight
Up from the cold ground they came so bright
With their flowers to blooming white
And leaves of green a beautiful delight

The daffodil the flower it be
Telling us that spring will be coming for thee
Even in an overnight snow squall
They stand beautiful and tall

Overnight they seem to appear
Not very good food for the local deer
For they are a forecaster of coming spring
With the return of the summer birds on wing

Seeing the daffodils stirs my mind
Of a happening way before my time
Of a event that changed the world of yours and mine
An open tomb and a love so divine

The opening of the daffodils bloom
As angels opened the Savior tomb
A stranger in the garden that morning
Women's glee and not mourning

I have heard of this event many a time
Yet fresh it is each time, for His love so divine
Freeing me from my sinful ways
Guiding me in His Way, day by day

Thank you God for the forecast of the for coming of spring

Buzz

Stained glass window

A stained glass window is a beautiful thing
Makes me think of Spring
The brightest colors I behold
With colorful glass a story told

It sits in a prominent place
Sometimes framed with fancy lace
Letting light in through its colored glass
Telling a story that will always last

A stained glass window does inspire me
To think of the event it does portray
In glass and lead it comes alive
As colored light is captured by my eyes

The story it tells may be Biblical or not
Or words that evoke a deeper thought
Told in color shining bright
As glass reflection the sun's eternal light

Warming colors and light that warm the soul
Telling me of a story or words in glass it beholds
This one below of words said long ago
By a man who came to save my soul

He spoke these words now set in glass
That guides us out of our sinful past
And that can lead us to follow His Way
Through the darkness into the light of day

The stained glass gives me a feeling of inner peace
Calming my body and mind; a pleasant release
For those words they do comfort my soul
Making me closer to God and feeling whole

Thank You God for the words in the stained glass window

Buzz

Summer's End

The long days of Summer have almost passed
We wish the Summer days could longer last
But there is a slight change in the air
The weather is turning pleasant and fair

Slight changes some seen and other not seen
For the season of Fall is about to enter the scene
The night creeps into the day's light
Shortening the day's light creating a longer night

Plants and trees have mostly met their maturity
As their fruits reach their maximum level of growth
For the harvest is close, close at hand
As Summer ends and Fall is about to expand

Leaves are beginning to change color and Fall to the ground
Most of the grasses have turned golden brown
Some of the Summer birds have left the scene
The squirrels prepare its nest for the winter's blustery scream

For many things the end of Summer will bring
Back to school some rejoice others a horrible thing
Vacations are done, gone is Summer fun
Back to work where work is never really done

But why this time of change
Maybe to prepare us for a different game
A time to prepare for the events to come
Of the harvests joys and the birth of a Son

God in His Wisdom has given us so much
A time for fun, harvest and such
And to remember the gifts and the Way to Follow
His Son and the Glory of life that has come

**Thank you God for Your creation, Your Son
and the changing of the seasons**

Buzz

Summer Full Moon

The sun has almost reached the horizon
Slowly setting on the western side
Taking its light slowly as it slowly
Slides away beneath the western sky

Daylight becomes the dusk of day
Streaking across the clouds painting them pink and gray
Finally the night has fully come
For the darkness of total night has begun

Then silently it will rise in the eastern sky
A summer full moon shining bright
No fanfare to start its display
As it follows an invisible track across the twinkling night sky

Its light the soul reflection of the sun
That bathes the land in a different tempered light
Winding through the leaves of the trees it goes
Making an ever changing design on the land below

That summer full moon has a warming glow
As it travels through the night
Sometimes peaking though a cloudy sky
Always watching as the land slowly passes below

God gave us the moon to light the nighttime darkness
Letting us know the Son is always there
For the light of the Son is shining through
To take away our darkness and despair

For we, as followers of the Way, are like the moon
Absorbing and reflecting the Son's light
With the help of Holy Spirit as we follow His Way
Bringing His light to the darkness every day

Thank you God for the Light, may we always reflect your Glory

Buzz

Sun and Son

It starts the day as it rises in the east
Spreading its golden rays to the western skies
Warming the land as it passes on high
Bringing light to the darkness, to the night, good by

He came to us as a baby long ago
Bringing light and hope to an oppressed soul
Enlightening the law in His own special way
Not the letter of the law but the spirit obey

Its light is always there as we circle its orb
Giving light and energy to earth where we do reside
Giving us seasons and years that pass
Constantly there its light, will always last

He came as the Son of the Most High
To teach us a new way to fly
With the Spirit of God deep inside
An eternal flame that once lit will not die

Nourishing the earth with its rays of light
Making each day sunny and bright
Dipping beneath the western sky
To appear in the morning after our rest we do apply

His presence does lighten the night and day
As He showed us a new Way
He died and rose for us and took our sins
And lives within us as the Holy Spirits wind

**Thank you God for nourishing of your
Son and sun, the everlasting light**

Buzz

Tables

A table is a piece of furniture we see
Standing tall on legs as sturdy as can be
Mainly four yet some tables have more
Always firmly planted on the floor

With a top as flat as flat can be
Very seldom the top do we see
For mainly it is covered with lots of stuff
Like papers, pens, books, and occasionally a winter muff

They come in many shapes and sizes
Some plain, others elegant taking the prizes
Others old and stately, some as modern as can be
All functional, society very important key

There is one table very important you see
With a very special setting it be
Only two elements are seen
Bread and wine or grape juice is upon the scene

I speak of a Communion Table; a wondrous sight
With a invisible guest serving with delight
Of His Body: the bread that gives us life day after day
And His Blood, the wine to cleanse our sins away

Thank You God for the Table that is showing us the Way

Buzz

Thanksgiving

It comes in the month of November
Not to be confused with a month they call December
A time to think of the blessings of the past
And the blessings that we have that last

For the harvest that came from the vine
For us to partake as we dine
As we reflect on the year that is almost gone
And prepare for the winter long

Thankfully we think of this November
Of all the gifts we have received
Of the wealth that has come our way
Be it on a gloomy or sunshiny day

Thanksgiving wealth can be in many forms
Family, home, work, play and more
Coming to us each and every day
Filling us with life, definite not a boring way

For the blessing we have come from above
For God our creator filled us with, His compassion and love
Gives to us what we can handle day by day
Each gift in God's particular giving way

For God's blessings are a Thanksgiving every day
Filling our lives with Love from Above
Helping us cast our worries and sin away
Leading us forth to the next beautiful, glorious day

We need to remember God's gift to us
That comes daily for in God we do trust
And to honor Him in our daily way
Following His Son's example day by day

Thank You God for Your Blessings every day

Buzz

The Bible

The Bible is a Book of many books
Tells stories and events of old
Filled with pages of adventure and mystery I know
Tales of violence and peace unfold

Telling stories of man and womankind
Tales a many of all sorts and kinds
Tales of vessels on stormy seas
Adventuring to lands not previously seen

Stories of the creation of time
Fill the pages with beauty sublime
Tales of the beginning of mankind
Where we started and why we die

Trials of the flesh and mind as will
Pitting strength against intelligence, so swell
Stories of prophets some young, some old
Tell of things we should have done so bold

Wars and captivity, temples on high
Furnaces and famine and flights to afar
Basket in waters and down city walls
And to a land where honey does flow

Stories of a baby who came in a cave so small
Wise men and Shepard's who came to the stall
Stars that shine brightly on a glorious night
Angelic choirs from heaven, a wondrous sight

Trips through the field of gains for to eat
A wedding and a wilderness event it shares
Feeding many with little but bread and fish
Preaching to hundreds or on a dirt floor and mat

Parade thought the city so shiny and bright
Destroying money tables both left and right
Sharing a meal with twelve on Passover day
Going to a garden, a place for to pray

Stories of followers following His clue
Telling people of what is new
Spreading the Word both hither and yon
Writing from prison to spread the Way far and beyond

The Bible a Book of books you see
Telling stories of people like you and me
How they did fall and rise again
To maybe rise and fall many times more

The book's stories end in many a way
Sometimes bad and sometimes good that day
Filled with inspiration and thought for thee and from Thee
Leading us on the very correct Way you see

The message it gives us both big and small
Is that God is there for one and for all
Sharing His creation ever today
With forgiveness forever and even the next day

**Thank You God for the Bible You inspired
and the stories You gave**

Buzz

The Book

I saw this book the other day
In a leather binding on display
A little tattered around its edges
With its cover a little worn, looking a little forlorn

Picking it up and I found it was not heavy like most
Opening up its papers so shiny and bright
Its pages sparkled in the light
The pages light to the touch as thin they be

This book is a book of many books you see
With many chapters in each book there be
Two main divisions called old and new
All written many years ago for me and you

The written words are of a time of old
Of a people and their quest to live true and bold
To the God they knew as The Only One
Who gave them a land of their own in the bright sun

It spoke to me of travels and wars
Times of plenty and times of no more
Men and women some good, some bad
Filling the pages with events some sad, others glad

Prophets and kings the stories the book does tell
Of babies, shepherds, and ladies quite well
Sons and daughters, in-law and some outside the laws
All of their trials and glories that the book recalls

This book I find is about life's everyday tales
Of the lives of mankind as they lived day by day
Trying to please God in their own human way
As relevant today as they were in those other days

Above all the book does tell of God's care
For the ones He does love so fair
He gives them choices to go their own way
Forgiving them for their wrongs they display

His rules are few and practical they be
To love one another as He loves thee
For the book's pages are filled with forgiveness and love
From our Father, Creator in Heaven Above

Thank you God for Your Book that guides our Way

Buzz

The Bowl

The day of Passover was coming soon
Streets were filling up as it was getting close to noon
Hearing the people from my place in the room
Not knowing what this Passover might bring

Years past I have had unleavened bread inside
Other times the bitter herbs I have held
So what is in store for me this year?
Sometime to savor I wait for the prize

They came early to set up for the meal that day
Low tables and cushions were scatted around
Dishes and goblets all set in place
But I was placed on a shelf far away

The guests came up the stairs and took their places
Then the meal came out as prescribed long ago
The leader stood up but something was wrong
He looked around, then He stared straight at me

He took me from my perch and a pitcher of water He found
Taking off His outer garments and used a towel as a sash
Water was placed in me almost to the top
A little cool but that was alright

Kneeling down to His companions He did go
Cleaning their feet of the dust that they wore
Then drying them off with the towel at His waist
Each in turn down the line He did go

But one named Peter said "not my feet"
He did wash Peter's feet and dried them that day
Telling them to be servants along the Way
To be a servant to all day after day

I was now filled with the dust of their feet
Then set aside as the blessing was said
The meal was partaken with words from the leader I heard
Tell of things to come as the dusk comes near

They left after the meal, they said for a place to pray
For now I was alone for the meal was done
But I remember back as He held me so firm
The warmth from His hands kept me steady that day

I felt rather special to be held that way
Holding the water that washed the feet that day
And listening to the leader as He told them of things
Being a part of a Passover meal, a new thing He did

I may be a bowl, to some an insignificant thing
Yet He made me feel special as I held the water that day
I guess we are all special in some unique way
For I understand I served the Lord: what a day

The owner came and cleaned the room
He found me on my shelf still filled with water so brown
Out the window the water did go
Then back on my shelf to sit all alone

We all have our place in this world they say
Some very large, others small and far away
Yet we all are important to God in some way
Hopefully fulfilling God's plan day after day

**Thank you Lord of those who feel insignificant
they are important to You**

Buzz

The Bud

Spring has come once again
The night darkness is shrinking
Daylight time is lengthening
Warmth of the days is spreading

Buds appear on the trees and bushes
Flowers emerge from the now warming ground
Small at first, the buds cling to a branch
For now nourishment flows to their very tips

Tightly wrapped from the cool morning chill
They slowly unfold as the day's warmth appears
More hearty they become as the sun earlier does arise
Soon they will be fully immersed in the day

They brighten up the day as they change the landscape
The world of winter that seems so bleak and cold
Has become a world of green, colors and warmth
Colors abounds as the buds blooms forth in many hues

Our Christian life is like the blooming buds
For God is our support, the branches on which we stand
His Son, Jesus is the nourishment, the Way
With the Trinity we may blooms and be fruitful

**Thank you God, as buds may we bloom
forth as part of Your creation**

Buzz

The Table

I stand in the dining room all covered with
bills, homework, pencils and pens
My sturdy four legs hold up my top so flat and secure
I yearn for the time I was surrounded and blessed
Like the first year I was new to this house
Remembering the time surrounded by laughter and guests
Not covered with bills, home work and such
Yearn for the time, I remember it well, of being covered in linen
Yes fine linen of grandmother's antique white table cloth
Upon the white linen they placed placemats for a setting of nine
The china came out all clean and with a light blue design
Only seven were there so they had to get two more
Silverware so shinny and bright; two forks, two
spoons and of all thing a butter knife
Cloth napkins were all surrounded by rings
With name tags placed at each elegant setting above
But only eight named name tags did I recognize that day
The ninth was placed with 'special guest', a mystery that day
Oh how I yearn for that time again
In the center was placed a fall flower bouquet
The meal was almost ready to start as I counted but eight
Four of the family was all there plus two sets of grandparents
That made eight then there is but one more, but whom
My math is not always good but that makes eight
Where is the mystery guest I know not where

Then I heard the dinner bell ring
Requesting those to come and be seated at a place so prescribed
Dishes came out of the kitchen beyond
Hot and golden brown the turkey did arrive
With all of the other fixing put side by side
The meal was ready yet the final guest was not here
Then one of the grandfathers disappeared to who knows where
He came back with a tray, cups, juice and some bread
Saying a blessing as he turned to the empty chair
"Here's to you honored guest"
He broke the bread and passed it on
Then a small cup of juice to everyone
He said "we honor our guest the Lord on High for all we have
This day of the Thanksgiving, a feast and for the blessing we have"
The meal was fun with conversation a plenty
Coming up next was a special treat
Dessert and my favorite pumpkin pie so smooth and sweet
Boy do I wish someone would spill a small piece
Oh how I yearn for that time again
I felt something being placed on my top
Today's paper came with a flop
My day dream of the past had suddenly stopped
The rest of the evening passed as the evenings before
Lights went out and they all went to bed, I don't snore
Alone I am again with all my friends the chairs
Oh to be able to serve and be there again

I was suddenly alert to the fact that my top was all clear
Two people were stretching me from end to end
Inserting my leaves and making me longer again
Then it came out from a drawer that antique white linen cloth
It covered me up and once again I know
The Lord God on High would grace my table top again this day

**Thank you My Lord and Savior for all the
blessing given this day and always**

Buzz

The Chair

I am a table as you can see
Top flat and as smooth as can be
Most of the time covered with papers and such
Yet on several occasions the center of much

Thanksgiving, Christmas and Easter are times I enjoy
Surrounded by people enjoying the feast
For supporting them there are my fellow friends the chairs
Sturdy and comfortable, standing straight and so tall

There is always an empty chair for our guest the Lord of All
Empty is the place we would honor that day
The chair is at the head of the table a place to stay
Its arms and cushions were clean and bright

Then grandfather told one of the children to move that day
To the head of the table and stay
For now there was an empty chair in the middle of all
For now the Lord would sit in the midst of the family that day

I asked the chair how did it feel one day
'I was afraid' he said 'that I was not worthy to stay
My cushion was ragged and with a small rip on one side
One leg was a little shorter than the rest, so I wobble a bit'

'To have the Lord God astride for He decided to stay'
The chair said 'it was an honor and humbling this way
I was filled with a warm, gentle peace that is hard to describe
Even though I was tattered and short on one side'

'A feeling of love, peace and joy
Warmed me to the core of my wooden frame
Awaiting the day when He will return
Hope again I will be chosen to honor the Lord'

We all serve the Lord in many a way
Some in silence as the table and chair
Others with kindness, love and a grin
To serve is an honor we should do each day

Yet we should never forget The Lord God on High
He gives us life to share and explore no matter our shape or size
The wonders of His Creation from door to floor
Each in our own special way to honor the Lord, day after day

Thank You Lord God on High for sharing with us your creation

Buzz

The Earth

The earth is a wonder place to be
Marvelous things to see from sea to shining sea
It sits and spins and is suspended in space
Science says in the Goldilocks place

To us it is rather large
Yet it is a little larger than Mars
Just the right size for humans to survive
On a planet that is very wise

Different environments are for us to see
From a land filled with the tallest of trees
To a desert of nothing but sand and more sand
And plains where rows upon row wheat stand

Mountains tall and mountains small
Streams and rivers that hear the wild life call
Insects so small they are hard to see
We know a little about the social life, of a bumble bee

A very diverse place the Earth happen to be
And all things seem to work in harmony
All with a purpose be it land, sky or sea
To praise the Creator, on bended knee

God gave us this Earth where we all be
Then He told us to be stewards of all we see
To care for the land, animals and sea
Are home is Earth, a wondrous place for you and me

**Thank You God for creating our home,
the Earth and all its wonders
Buzz**

The Forest

Outside my window a forest came into view
For out there are trees old and new
Standing tall in brown and green
Spreading their branches and leaves throughout the scene

The forest stretches for quite a way
But my eyes see not as far even on a sunny day
For as I look out that forest way
My view was blocked by the leaves and branches on display

Through the canopy is the sky so blue
Framed by the branches and leaves that grow
Poking holes in the cluster of leaves so green
Silhouetting others of beauty now seen

The floor of the forest was covered with leaves and brush
Places for those who must hide to have lunch
Vines, twigs, brambles, and leaves cover the ground
Hiding those who do not want to be found

Ever changing day by day
And being a part of the season's display
Bare in the Winter, warmed by the Summer sun
Bursting forth in Spring. colorful leaves in the Fall, what fun

A home to many hiding in the trees
The deer with a coat of buckskin hard to see
A fox with cubs hidden in a den
Gray squirrel looking for acorns upon which he depends

A wonderful place the forest be
Filled with places and sights most do not see
Peaceful and quiet when first we come near
Yet filled with a new adventure when we see a deer

The forest does provide us with things we need
Materials to protect us from the wintery blast
Food and covering so we can last
And a place to consider nature as it slowly does pass

God created this forest I do see
Created a place where life is free
To live in beautiful harmony
A blessing for all of us to see

Thank You God for the forest so beautiful and free

Buzz

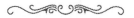

The Little Yellow Headed Finch

A little yellow headed finch came to visit today
She found the feeder filled with seeds yesterday
The feeder is a cylinder black and tall
With a circular perch for the feet so small

She hung on to the feeder upside down
Sampling the seeds of black, yellow and brown
Soon she was followed by some of her friends
All trying to get their fill at the black holey dinner bin

Watching them intensity I tried not to move
Counting as many as six at a time some grayish blue
All of a sudden awaythey all flew
Chirping and twittering of the seeds they now knew

God has given creation this beautiful bird
As we see it has no care in the world
Like the bird we need also be
Dependent upon God, for He gave us life you see

Thank You God for small creatures that depend on You

Buzz

The Moon

A mellow light crept over the eastern horizon
Illuminating the night with its silvery rays
Changing the night from darkness to a lighter display
Carrying on for the sun now gone away

Its silvery rays change the night to shadows on display
As the light threads its way through the trees and objects in its way
Ever changing shadows move across the ground
Creating colors only seen when the moon is around

What do I see with the moon on the rise
It's a light in the darkness shining brightly from above
A beacon that shows the traveler his way
God's light in the night overhead on display

He came to earth in the dead of night
Filling the darkness with His Light so bright
Guiding us towards a new Way while He leads The Way
Giving us new lessons to follow day after day

For darkness is the sins of man
His Light, like the moon, illuminates {The} (our) way
For He died and rose for us, taking our {sins} (darkness) away
(For) In darkness we will no longer stay

Thank You God for Your Son reflected in the night sky

Buzz

The Oak Leaves

They glisten in the sunlight
Shimmering their brilliant green so brightly
As the breeze tenderly moves them around
Dancing ever so gently almost without a sound

For spring is finally here
The once small buds have disappeared
Revealing the leaves so full and bright
Now nourishing the tree from the sun's light

The tree feeds the young leaf buds to start it to grow
Then the leaves return its sugar to the tree below
Working together they both survive
To live a long healthy time alive

From a small seed it grows and spreads
Weathering the storms, raising its head
Strong and resilient it branched out far
Spreading its branches and leaves over the land below

For God is like the tree
Strong, sturdy, and with love abound
Feeding His disciples and people all around
But only wanting praise and love in return

His message started long ago
To a tribe of people we all know
Then He sent His seed to show the Way
With branches and leaves here to stay

Thank You God for Your being our Creator and Guide

Buzz

The Phone

The phone is a device we have in tow
That has come about in the modern age I know
That keeps us in touch with those
Who have their devices also in tow

They come in my styles, you see
So important to holder they be
Communicating before dusk to beyond dawn
A companion that if without is like a death song

Some are smart and do all you need to do
Others simple and just talk or text to you
All are devices that keep us in touch
A device we have become a slave to, too much

We fret and stew if we are out of range
Consider the loss a great stress and pain
We wait for the next call or text to arrive
Needed to communicate to other even if they are by our side

Yet there is one who does not need a phone
For He will never put us on hold or leaving us alone
The line we have is a direct line you see
Be it night or day His line is always open to you and me

For prayer needs no phone to converse
Just talk to God, you may even try some verse
For God is there night or day
Listening to our prayers, no phone we need to display

Thank You God for always having an open line

Buzz

The Return

In the days to come
As Jesus returns to claim
Those of us who call Him King
We Trust God to be our guide

When will He come we do not know
In the dark of night or morning glow
So we prepare for the time
Our life we must keep in tow

We try to follow the teaching of the Way
Trying to be followers day by day
Reading and learning the Biblical way
And trying to apply them yet today

For we know He will come
We hope we are prepared for the day
Our glorious King will come and stay
And we are there for that wondrous day

Thank You God for preparing us for Your Son's return

Buzz

The Rose

Looking out my window I see a rose
As beautiful as can be
A plant that was not planted by me
But has grown there for many a year you see

This rose came from a single bud
That burst forth with petals in the summer's sun
In a glorious yellow color it came
That only nature can explain

It sits upon a rose bush so green
With leaves as dark green as green can be
Protected by its thorns so sharp and fine
Attracting the insects to come and dine

This single rose is not alone you see
With other roses upon the same bush they be
Bursting forth their petals on display
Saying how glorious is this lovely day

I forget the wonders of nature around me
Until I see that rose where it be
Spreading its petals for all to see
Alive in the world of nature for you and me

God created this rose and others I see
With many colors and shapes they be
Showing the world the glory of God
For the wonders of nature is God's eternal, everlasting Love

Thank You God for the simple beauty and message of Your rose

Buzz

The Silk Tree

We have a silk tree out in our yard
A gift from a friend gone afar
Several years older it has grown in a unique way
Two large branches head up to heaven you see

Leaves are green like other trees be
Yet they look like fans of a palm tree
Seven pairs of leaves on each stem there are
Each with many little green fingers out stretched so far

The flower they are of a most delicate delight
Like a miniature puff fans they spread in the sunlight
The tips of the flowers have a brilliant red glow
The rest of the flower is white as snow

Hummingbirds like the red flowers glow
For sweet nectar is hiding there they know
For God has created this beautiful sight
One beautiful tree against an ocean blue sky and clouds of white

Thank You God for all your creations including the silk tree

Buzz

The Sounds

What do I hear
The world around comes to my ear
Filling me with words and sounds
A cacophony of sounds that continue to resound

A jumble of noise loud and clear
Wonder where all those sounds come from to my ear
Blending in a way which is hard to keep clear
All these sounds coming to my ear

I took a little time to listen to all those sounds
Filtered out the sound I knew so profound
Gone were the sounds of cars on their way
And the sound of an airplane cruising the skyway

When all the known sounds were filtered away
The sound of nature has not gone way
For in those sounds I heard God on display
Nature had returned like a brand new day

But then I realized of all the sounds I have heard
All are sounds of God and of His Creation Word
City noises that fill my ear
Nature's songs that I think are far are really near

I realized that the sound of God's Creation is all that I hear
Be them cars or children at play, be they far or near
In the city or country scene
All are God's Creations from a God Supreme

Thank You God for Your creation and all Your sounds

Buzz

The Storm

This morning's sky was covered with a canvas blue
But in the west clouds begin to loom
Filling in the sky from west to east with a white cover
Slowly again the sky darkened starting in the west

Filling the sky with an ominous darkness
Cooling the air as a breeze came forth
Birds seek shelter from the oncoming storm
Slowly it came as a single raindrop fell from above

The ground is slowly changing from
Light sun dried tan to shadow tan as storm clouds formed
For rain will slowly moisten the ground's exposed topsoil
As more and more fall they darken the ground below

The first big drops create small craters in the dusty dry ground
Spraying water and dust all around
Hitting with a plopping resound
Nourishing the ground with a splashing sound

Bigger drops now fall from on high
Hitting the ground and pavement with a splash
Bouncing up to fall one last time
Covering the ground with its clear liquid shine

Raindrops fall on leaves and plants of green
First clinging onto the dry surface green, with more drops
Then slipping down and falling to the earth below
Hitting the ground with a gentle splat

Weakened leaves stricken by the rain flutter downward
Painting the ground with their wet glossiness
Creating an unique pattern of leaves over leaves
Protecting the ground from the steady falling rain

The storm lasted several hours
Drenching the ground with life giving rain
Creating puddles and ground of dark brown
Nourishing the ground with its life giving water

Small streams of water meander down the hill
Bumping into pebbles that divert their path
Filling unseen depressions with their pooling water
Bringing with them small pieces of dirt

Slowly the rain lessened its falling
Fewer and fewer drops streaked to the ground
The clouds began to lighten on the western horizon
As a sliver of blue stretched it's way eastern

Dark clouds changed to light gray then white
Slowly they disappeared over the eastern horizon
Patchy is the sky of white and blue
Letting the sun shine through

Following the storm and filling the sky
The bright colors of a rainbow arches on high
Reminding us of a promise as old as can be
That God is there for you and me

**Thank you God for the storms and the precipitation
that cools and nourishes Your creation.**

Buzz

The Tomb

In a garden not far from the city
I am a tomb in the side of a hill
Empty and dark in silence I be
A tomb for a nobleman new and not used

I was carved into this hillside
Much stone was removed to created me
My chamber fairly large yet room for only one
A tomb for an important person in a peaceful garden

Alone I stood for many a day
Empty, cool and dark did I stay
The days passed by and Passover came its way
Pilgrims passed through the garden to the city beyond

Sounds from the city could be heard nearby
As the Passover feast week came to a close
Jeers from the city filled the air
And the faint sound of metal on metal could be heard

At midday the sky turned dark and then almost black
A little later my chamber did quake
Rocks on the hillside came loose and tumbled down
To the foot of my opening, some splitting in two

Then later that day a procession draw near
Carrying a man all bloody and bruised; not my owner
Into my chamber they lay him down then
Someone covered his lifeless body with white linen burial cloth

They left in a hurry for night drew near
A large stone was pushed over my opening
To seal us in this cool and once empty space
Alone we were in silence for we spoke not a word

That night did pass and another one too
As the third day began I felt something move
The stone at my entrance suddenly moved
For an angel or two were now sitting astride

Guards outside my entrance were suddenly amazed
They stood like statues at the sight of those brilliant angels
Then fled to the city with hats in hands
Never to be seen or heard from again by me

The inside of my chamber was now as bright as the sun
Two angels came in and bid him to rise
The man in my chamber rose up and went outside
Then folding the linens the angels sat down inside

Visitors came early that morning
To prepare the body for the passing on
He was not to be found in my tomb you see
They thought someone had carried him away. not me

But I knew what had happened that early morning
That man was not dead he was alive that day
Fulfilling a prophecy of one foretold
For the temple of God, in three days would it be restored

Many more visitors came to me to see what had happened
Some rejoiced to see an empty tomb
Others doubted what they did see
That day I will remember, for I know the truth, ask me

The man they laid inside me
Only stayed but two days within my walls
He rose to life after being crucified days before
Showing mankind the Way and forgiving mankind's sins evermore

**Thank You God for Your Son who died
and rose to shows us the Way**

Buzz

He is risen!
He is risen indeed!

The Waves

I saw a small portion of the lake from my window this day
Its waves slowly meet the rocky shore below
Lapping over the rocks in the water just above the surface
Then slipping over the wet other side and then meet the shore

Rhythmically they came to their journey's end
In an ever moving rhythmic score
Retreating as the next wave came behind it
Dashing or lapping itself upon the rocky shore

Sunlight touched the crest of the on-coming waves
Changing its blue to an almost invisible shade
The rocky surface below the water is sunlight clear
Being bathed in the warmth of the new morning light

This day was a calm day as the waves came
Yet the other day the wind did blow
Creating white caps on the wave's tops like a winters snow
That beat the shore again and again with a muted roar

God did create this scene I do see
A part of His creation; the water, the lake and the rocks that be
For the waves can be a lesson for you and me
Ponder and consider for life they could be

The waves are like one's life, sometimes calm and serene
Other times beating ourselves against a rocky dangerous shore
Yet calmness is there in the rhythm of life, for life must go on
If we trust in the Lord all will be right; calm as a gentle wave

**Thank you God for the waves on the shore
that shows us life forever more**

Buzz

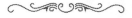

The Wind

Unseen, as it passes over land and sea
Moving leaves, grass, dust ever so slightly
Pushing them to new places
Sometimes gently, other times violently

Many a name this unseen event does have
Marriah, Gale, Breeze, Haboob, Zephyr
Crossing the land and sea all wild and free
As it fills the sails and rustles the leaves

It changes the land and sea as it passes by
Creating large waves at sea to ripples on a pond
Sculpturing the land into rocky displays
Spreading pollen that causes me to sneeze

Warming the land or cooling it down
Pushing the clouds across a blue canvas sky
Creating recognizable shapes then swishing them away
Driving the snow or rain on its way

Moving the windmills to grind the grain
Drying the sheets that hang down the lane
Lifting the kites as they sail on high
Letting the birds glide through the sky

Pushing the waves higher on Galilee
Warming that day as the wedding would be
Changing day into night on Calvary
Parting the waters of the Sea of Reeds

For God is like the wind
Unseen yet always present
Encouraging us gently at times, then swiftly at others
Surrounding us always with His Everlasting Love

**Thank you God for Your presencs like
the wind unseen yet felt by me**

Buzz

The World Around

Sitting outside the other day
I saw the world on display
An ever changing place to see
That was close and yet far away from me

For I live in the world of man
Trying to do what I can
To live from day to day
In this hurry-up world of mankind on display

With all its gadgets and stuff
Trying to keep up with it is really tough
Meetings, work, programs, projects and such
It seem as if there is not enough time, I go to much

Sitting outside what did I see
All of nature that surrounding me
Plants so beautiful grow without a care
Birds flying high in the air

A squirrel scampering up a tree
A red rose on a bush, so beautiful and delicate as can be
I saw a humming bird at a flower feeding nearby
Then twisting vines stretching up to the sky

Not a care in the world do they conceive
For above all God does provide for their daily needs
For day to day they do survive
Praising God is a part of their daily lives

For we should try to emulate nature around
Trusting in God for all we do needs is sound
Living from day to day like birds in the air
Praising God for the life we do share

For God has created nature and all
To share it on this bright blue ball
For there is a harmony in nature, we should follow true
By praising God on this day and the next so new

Thank You God for nature that gives us life day by day

Buzz

Thunder

At first it comes as a muffled boom
Far in the distance barely heard
As darker the clouds and sky become
Their rumbles come closer and clear to hear

The clouds bring the thunder and lightning
We hear and see the wondrously experience
A flash of light streaks across the sky
Followed by the clap of thunder from on high

Telling us that the storm is coming near
As it cools the air and rustles the leaves
Ever darkening the clouds and sky above
Then releasing its moisture to the land below

Life giving rain falls from above
Nourishing the land with its liquid love
Turning the ground from light brown
To a darker chocolate display

The first drops scatter the dust on the ground
Making small dents with a plopping sound
As they cover the land with droplets from on high
Falling so gently from high in the sky

More and more they come from on high
Filling the puddle and with its supply
Of life giving liquid so fresh and clean
Dripping from leaves, a beautiful scene

Then suddenly a flash and crack from above
As the thunder hastens rain to fall
To the land below to nourish it all
For the clouds must move on to spread its liquid love

The thunder begins to be a distant sound
Fading to low rumbles as the storm moves along
Taking its rain away for another day
To come again with a different thundering display

God nourishes His creation in many ways
Giving life and liquid in many wondrous displays
That cools the ground and lets flora and fauna grow
To provides us with life as we all know

Thank You God for the many ways to nourish Your creation

Buzz

Time

We live in a time when speed is the thing
Impatience fills our lives, we never seem to unwind
We must have it now to enjoy the day
No matter what it may cost, we pay

The latest devices come into sight
Beckoning us on to have the next delight
To be faster, swifter and more in control
And be one ahead of the man called Joe

We used to think that mail was so great
Travel by Model T was really first rate
The telephone a most delightful communication device
And flying in the air so very nice

Quickly they fade as time goes by
A second is now too slow we say
Our computers must respond in less time than that
We want an answer before the question is even asked

Quickly time does fly by these days
We check our devices to see where we are
As slaves to time and devices we have in hand
Wondering why we have no time to enjoy this land

Slaves to the devices we now use
So dependent we have no time for ourselves
Running here and there on the click of a watch
Wishing we had more time than on a clock

There is a solution to this furious pace
Put down that device and hide it someplace
Turn it off and go look at the sky
Relax and watch the clouds go by

If you must use the device here is something to do
Set aside some time for just family and you
Start small then increase it a few
Another thing is talk to the Lord, He will listen to you

God gave us these devices to use, not abuse
To make our lives easier not crowded and confused
To ease our lives along the Way
And keeps us following God everyday

**Thank You God for all those convenient devices,
may we use them properly and wisely**

Buzz

Time

Time the element that orders our lives
That keeps us on task as events fly by
It comes in a measured amount
Constantly moving forward as each second counts

We view time in many forms:
Minutes, seconds, hours, days,
Weeks, years, month and even decades
All in the forms to keep us in line

We may try to skip the click of the clock
But in this fast paced world we cannot
Can we make it stand still
Time says it is against its will

Its pace is steady and true
Moving on despite what we want to do
The hour will pass, sixty minute long, precisely, it will pass
Steady today and tomorrow as it did in the past

God gave us these units of time to use
He gave us time not to abuse
We have let time rule our world
Putting our lives in a constant whirl

His intent was to use time wisely
To take time to care for others' nicely
Using our time for those in need
And time for His creation and Him, yes indeed

**Thank You God for the elements of time, may
we be a good stewards of your time**

Buzz

Transition Time Dusk

Transition time, the time between day and night
When the sun has dipped below the horizon
The night has not begun
For now pale daylight still lingers

The world outside is a different place
The day birds no longer can be heard
For their once joyful songs are now silent
They have gone to rest

The sky is not black as night to come
But a pale blue, before the stars break through
For a silence has crept over the land
And the day creatures have headed to their rest

Flowers of the day slowly close their petals
Conserving the warmth of the day
A humming bird takes its last drink
Then retires to its nest in a tree not far away

What can be heard is a chorus of crickets
Singing the song of 'here I am'
As the pale light quickly fades away
Allowing the night to spreads it starry canvas overhead

The pace of life has slowed down
In preparation for the night's rest to begin
A time to reflect on the day passed
And maybe think about the day to come

For the transition from day to night is short
The stillness is magical as the day has ended
For calmness is covering the land
As the pale light fades into the darkness of night

God in His wisdom has created the dusk
For us to reflect on His glorious day just passed
And the wonders of His world before us
As we prepare to rest, for another new glorious day is to come

God help us to reflect on the glory of the day just passed

Buzz

Unique Moon

I saw the full moon the other night
Shining through the trees so bright
Bouncing and weaving its light through the leaves
Letting me see a sight I could not believe

The moonlight looked like a group of twinkling stars
Brighter than stars from afar
Sparking, as the moonlight danced through the leaves
Bring a spectacular light display hard to believe

A light breeze filled the night
Dancing with the leaves before the moonlight
A new dimension from the light of the moon
As the sparkling moonlight takes away the night's gloom

The very next night the moon did arise
I had hoped the same light show came before my eyes
To my disappointment it did not reappear again
That magic of that moment I will see, who knows when

God gave me that moment I did see
To impress upon me
The wonders of God's majesty
And that He created all the universe and me

Thank You God for that special moonlight You let me see

Buzz

Water

The life blood of Nature water be
It comes from the sky you see
Falling upon the land and sea
Giving nourishment to all that be

Water from the sky falls upon the land
Coming in many forms it can
Like snow in the winter clean and fluffy bright
Or dew in the morning reflecting the sunlight

Light Spring showers then a rainbow appears
Hail that comes down the size of a pea crystal clear
A summer thunder storm mighty not to fear
Sheets of raindrops with thunder in the ear

Soaking into the ground and then to a stream
Giving life to the land as it covers the scene
With its life giving liquid that makes plants green
Following a course to the sea or the ocean scene

It fills our body with fluid that flows
From the tip of our toes to the end of our nose
Giving us life to keep us on the go
Keeps us clean and protects us from diseases unknown

I came across a man the other day
A man of peace I encountered on my way
Who gave me a drink of water He had
That cleansed my soul and made me glad

For the water He gave is the most precious to me
The Living Water from my Lord you see
The everlasting water that is love of Him
That cleanses my soul and makes me closer to thee

Thank You God for the Living Water from Your Son

Buzz

We Age

We all age from the day we were born
Spreading our wings as we first step forth
Counting the hours to age a little bit more
Awaiting the day we can be on our own

We pass through the years wondering if
We will reach what we want, we set in the sky
Wiser we get as years go by
Still following that star we set in the sky

As time passes we begin to slow down
For the teens, twenties and thirties are past
Can we remember them well?
For then we had the ambition to follow our star

The forties and fifties passed with a flash
We have met a lot of people but some have moved on
But memories still linger of them to this day
Beckoning back to how we did play

As we sit and watch what's on TV
Answering those questions on Jeopardy with a breeze
Realizing that we did not forget that
After all our minds are filled with stuff far back

The body is older but our mind moves on
We only need to remember one thing or is it a song
And that would be; you are as young as you think you are
A blessing to be sure for thee and we

God gave us this body and mind to explore
The wonders of His Kingdom from floor to floor to floor
It doesn't matter if we don't go far
As long as you try to follow Him through that open door

God gave us this time and place on this Earth
To grow and be nourished by His Word
The body may be old but the mind must say
Live for today as a young child of God: the only Way

Thank you God for the time to age and follow your Way

Buzz

Wealth

Wealth, a word with many facets
Mainly we think about assets
How much do I have today
Is it close at hand or far away

Should I impress my friends
Showing it off as to what I have to spend
Try with my wealth to influence my way
Or hide it in a safe place for another day

Yet wealth is more than money in hand
The poor can have wealth, they can
Dignity and self pride, wealth they be
For self-esteem is an important wealth you see

A loving family is wealth for me
Caring about each other, a family be
Sharing the load as well as the pain
Respecting one another, so we all gain

Knowledge is wealth, a blessing to have
Knowing what to do makes me glad
Sharing wisdom with those in need
Knowing when to be silent and when to say please

My health is a wealth I cherish a lot
To get from here to there and hitting that spot
To be able to get up every day
And to see another glorious day on display

For there are many other forms of wealth's for us to find
Each has his or her own wealth to define
Filling our lives day after day
Enhancing our lives and others as we pass this way

Yet there is one wealth I hold above all the rest
The wealth of spirit I have for Christ, the very best
Who provides for me through thick and thin
And He died and rose for my terrible, unspeakable sins

Thank You God for the many wealth's You have given me

Buzz

A Beam

What am I doing here?
As a tree I was to be a keel in a large boat
My dream was to be a beam in a splendid palace
But now I am in a pile with other beams

What am I doing here?
Pulled from the pile I was mated
With another piece of the tree I once was
My mate was placed near the middle of my frame

What am I doing here?
They pulled me out with two others like me
Setting us aside as I wondered what would be
Then a soldier drug us out, I saw prisoners three

What am I doing here?
I was placed on the shoulder on one of the men
And he carried me away with soldiers as guards
Through the streets of Jerusalem as I thumped along

What am I doing here?
I could tell I was heavy on this man
As I weighted heavy on his shoulder he prodded on
He fell to the street and I fell with a loud thump

What am I doing here?
On he went, yet a second time this man did fall
Again I fell with a loud thump to chears of the crowd
Almost crushing the man as I fell once more

What am I doing here?
A man from the crowd was took to take his place
Then all three of us headed up the street to the hill
I heard them called the hill, the Skull, I know not why

What am I doing here?
On reaching the crest of the hill I was laid flat
Cold was the ground, a little muddy too
Then the man was laid flat on me on his back

What am I doing here?
I felt a sharp pain in my frame
For a soldier was nailing this man to my beam
The pain increased as the nail went deeper and deeper

What am I doing here?
I could hear the man moan in pain as the hammer did strike
Then the other wrist was secured, his pain I felt
Then his feet were nailed together in a similar way

What am I doing here?
They then lifted me up and slid me into a hole
As I hit the bottom I stopped with a jolt
The man nailed to me felt the shock of my sudden stop

What am I doing here?
I could feel his pain as he hung from my frame
Wishing I could do something to ease his plight
Watching and waiting as the day suddenly was night

What am I doing here?
They nailed a sign over his head that day
Which said; The King of the Jews
That man died on me that very day

What am I doing here?
Some people took him down; carried him away
I was alone once again with his blood on my frame
Wondering what all this did mean that day

The man that was crucified on my beam
Was the King of all Kings!
Later I heard that he rose from the dead
They say he died for all that day

For I have become a symbol after that day
A cross of injustice and life they say
For the man I held that day
Died to save us all from our sins for eternity

What am I doing here?
For I was the beam that held an innocent man
A King who died so that all can understand
That the Son of God died for all that day

His death, saved us all from sin
To show us the Way we can follow
To the Creator and God above all
The one and only the Great I Am

Thank you God for the cross that bears our sins and the light

Buzz

What is a Church?

The Church is where the religious faithful may be
Gathering there to listen, pray and learn
Some places are magnificent to see
Others outside, just a tent they may be

Some say a building shiny and bright
Filled with stained glass; a wondrous sight
Paintings of old on the ceiling above
Sculptures of saints or of people they love

A glorious place they say where God would be
Goblets and ornaments of silver and gold
Elegant chandeliers casting their light below
A place of beauty to behold

Some say a cellar down below
Away from the eyes of those who don't know
Lit with candles to warm and brighten the dark site
Chairs in rows are framed in the dim light

Spartan in its setting yet functional it be
For a community of faithful, a church it be
Filling the needs of any group gathered here
Sharing the lessons of the Bible so near

Church buildings come in many sizes
From mega buildings to places for but possibly only five
In homes, in old firehouses, basements and such
They all serve as places to gather for worship, a must

But these are but buildings or place they assemble
For where they gather is not the church but the people within
Who move outside to the world beyond
Spreading the joy of lessons so learned

Helping the less fortunate both far and wide
Visiting the infirmed by their bedside
Giving a hand to a stranger in need
Giving the birds and creatures their winter-feed

The church is people here, far and wide
Who follow the lessons heard inside
To spread the joy of the Word far and wide
Hopefully making this world a more peaceful place

Thank you God for Your Words that we can follow day after day

Buzz

What is Stewardship

The time has come again
When we must think of where we're been
Of things that have happened
And where we want to be

Did we do it right or pass it on
Could we have done more with what we have
Or let ride, like what we have done before
It is time to look at our box once more

It is said we should look outside of the box
Some say try something new
But first we must look inside
At self and see, have we really done, what there is to do

Have we done our share or passed it on
Let someone else go beyond
Only we can answer that true
It is between God and you

So think about the time at hand
Are we doing the best we can
Be it volunteer and or money in hand
To serve God in this time and in His land

Thank You God, may I be the best steward to You I can

Buzz

Where is Spring?

In the midst of Winter with snow on the ground
I yearn for Spring to come around
To fill my days with joy and fun
And bask in the warmth of the Spring time sun

The trees are sparse with a few leaves of brown
Most have fallen to the ground
The branches on which they hung
Are mostly bare where once bird songs were sung

The sun tries to brighten the day
Only to accent their naked branches on display
For in the distance the mountains seen to say
With snow on top Winter seem to be here to stay

Winter coats are worn by all
Put on in the late days of fall
Protecting all from the Wintry blast
Surely this cold will not last

For Spring will come that is a fact
When Winter has its last cold act
Flowers will feel the warmth of the sun
In days to come Winter will be done

For the hope in Winter is that Spring is near
For Winters cold will one day disappear
As the warmth of Spring is getting near
Some more of Winter we must endure

As sunlight gets stronger every day
We know that Spring is on its way
Melting the snow and warming the rain
Soon Winter will not be a strain

God gave us the Winter to prepare
Lent and Easter are in the air
To celebrate and prepare for life's rebirth
For our Risen Lord's Kingdom is here on Earth

**Thank You God for the anticipation of
Spring with a renewed beginning**

Buzz

Wild Flowers

Did Spring come early this year
Or did I just want Spring to be here
The wild flowers did they come early
For some I saw when the snow was still near

A wild flower is a thing of joy
Heralding that Spring is near
It brightens the day in the cool Spring sun
Colors to cheer for Spring has begun

Some even beat the migrating birds
Delicate yet hardy they defy a storm
Reaching heavenward in glorious form
Drinking in the God's sun and rain

For God has provided for this glorious flower
He cares for it each and every hour
If He can do that for a wild flower in Spring
His Love will care for us, even more

Thank you God that you care for us more than wild flowers

Buzz

Winter Approaches

These late Autumn days are different than past days
Some leaves are still on the trees
Most have fallen yet still some linger on
They cover the ground as a carpet of yellow and brown

Yet in the breeze there was something unique
The breeze though gentle was different I say
More of a chill I did feel as the breeze passed my way
Rustling the leaves as it blew that day

The sky was overcast as clouds passed slowly by
Turning the sky a mournful gray
Hiding the warmth of the sun on high
Making me think it might bring the rain our way

The darkness comes earlier these days
Lengthening the night and into the morning it does stay
Cooling the days for Winter is not far away
As a familiar sounds fill the late Autumn days

The sounds of wings on high,
Leaves rustling on the ground as a deer pass by
The thud of acorns as they fall to the ground
Or the sound of an Autumn rain as it comes down

The beauty we see and hear is fleeting
For the colors and sounds of Autumn cannot stay
Winter and its time to rest is coming soon
For the harvest is done, with the Harvest moon

And who do we owe this season we see
Our Creator of the universe He be
He gave us the seasons to enjoy and prepare
The Giver of life and seasons to share

Thank You God for the Autumn and the seasons to come

Buzz

Canyon Lands Winter

A canyon in winter is a magnificent display
Shining brightly on a winter's day
Rocky canyons narrow and tall
Hoping a rock does not fall

Layer upon layer they stretch to the sky
Some like mighty castles hard to deny
Canyons and ravines cut the rocky scene
Deep into the mountainside with trees between

The winter snow sprinkles the scene
Covering some, leaving others bare and clean
As the day's sun melts the snow on the ridges up high
The cold air freezes the melt to a beautiful ice fall by and by

The ice falls cling to the walls, a beautiful display
Growing by night, shrinking by day
Working its icy way down from the rocky ledge
Trying to reach the next rocky edge

God created this canyon and more
For the eyes to see and explore
Over many years He has carved this scene on display
Ever changing day after day

**Thank You God for the canyon scene
created by Your Almighty Hand**

Buzz

Winter is Here

The season called Winter has arrived
It slid in sometime during Christmastime
Showing up after the Fall was done
Bringing a new color to the land all around

The colors are of a subdued scheme
With brown leaves and trees dulled by the Winter scene
And gray seems to always be on display
Offset by brilliant white snow on a cold sunny day

The sun is low in the southern sky
Arriving late on the eastern horizon side
Leaving early as the night arrives
Trying to warm the earth as it struggles to get high in the sky

Its days are counted as gloomy, not bright
Yet some days are a warm delight
Some days a clear blue sky accent its mountains of white
While snow covers the fallen leaves out of sight

The cold of Winter chills the day
Its rain is cold and its wind bites when it blow this way
Winter is a time to prepare and relax
Springtime will come; that is a fact

God created this season in which we now reside
To remember a Royal Birth and a New Year just passed by
A time to celebrate the birth of a King
And a new year with new beginning it brings

In Winter we access the past and prepare for new days to come
For God has given us a time to start anew
To reenergize our lives with the birth of His Royal Son
In Wintertime our new life has begun, the past is done

**Thank You God for Winter and a time
to reflect and move forward**

Buzz

Winter Night

A Winter night is on unique time
The longer nights of Winter trick the mind
Telling you it is time to rest
Time to head to your nice warm nest

Shorter daylight keeps you inside
Where we want to stay there, on the warmer side
Away from the dark and Winter storms
The howling winds, the wet and cold of the Winter's bite

Winter nights last long into the morning
Ending the day with early dawning
Shorter mornings making for a gloomy beginning
Knowing that the day light will have a quick ending

Yet there are delights in a Winter's night
The snow on the ground, a crunchy delight
The steam clouds from your mouth billowing forth
A chill on your cheek as the north winds blow

The sight of snowflakes drifting slowly to the ground
And the silence of the Winter night all around
The full moon shining brightly in the cold dark night
Reflecting off the snow making the Winter night slivery bright

For on a Winter night time may pass slowly
Memories come of times and events, some of them holy
Christmas passed begin to fill the mind, some of long ago times
For the real meaning of Christmas is there in your mind

For on that Winter's night, the Bible says
A boy child was born and laid down his head
In a manger of straw as his cradle be
His birth brought strangers near, far and wide to see

For the boy baby born that Winter night
Brought forth a very special light
A light that would turn the world around
Who's words and actions around the world would resound

For as tradition does say on that Winter's night
A Savior was born to a virgin bright
Who will go on to save the souls of man
And bring a peace to mankind and the land

**We Thank You God for the Winter nights to
reflect on Christmas as wonderful delights**

Buzz

Winter Scene

I looked outside at a winter scene
For now we are in the season of in-between
The beauty of Fall and the new growth merging in Spring
They both do their colorful beauty thing

The trees outside seem withered and worn
Branches reaching out nude and forlorn
Most leaves have left their branches on high
Leaving clear paths to the sky

Some leaves still hanging on tight
In spite of the winter's windy might
Others twisting in the winter winds
Dancing to an unknown song with a leafy brown skin

Within the trees and branches life is there
Protected deep within the trees so bare
Waiting out the winter's cold and snow
For the warmer spring and buds to grow

For within us there is that bud of life
Dominate within our world of sin
Until we let Christ come in
For then our new life will begin

For in the winter scene, God has given us time to think
Our sins are as bare to God as the winter trees
We only need to take responsibility you see
And follow the example of His Son to set us free

Thank You God for the winter scene Your Son and His Way

Buzz

Printed in the United States
By Bookmasters